HTML 5 Visual Learning

a comprehensive example set for getting up to speed fast

Mike Ludo

Code Blaze Books
Vancouver, British Columbia, Canada
Copyright 2020

www.codeblazebooks.com

ISBN 978-1-7770267-0-7

Note

This book is **published in black and white** to keep the price down. Examples that use color **rely on the provided code** to present the color information once you execute the HTML script in your code editor.

Table of Contents

Preface

The *HTML 5 Visual Learning Guide* fills a gap in the learning and reference works on introductory web design. Instead of the terse definitions written for experts found in online documentation resources, or long commentaries to ease novices into programming, this volume strikes a balance between succinct explanation and complete visualizations of code so that the key concepts are learned through easy-to-follow examples. This book assumes no previous knowledge of HTML, web development or programming. If you do have some experience with setting up a website, by uploading source code text files and resources to directories on a server via an ftp client application, then you can skip or skim through the Introduction and move on to the main Tags and Elements section.

Introduction

Access the Code Files

All the code in this book can be downloaded or copied from a Google doc so that you can save a little time typing and follow along with the examples a little faster. However, the more time you spend typing, the better and faster you will learn how to write HTML! So therein lies a bit of a conundrum. The link to all the code in the following pages is

```
http://bit.ly/allCode
```

In the Google doc, all the code referenced in the following pages can be quickly found by clicking on its associated tab in the Google doc outline at the left of the screen (shown below). Just go to the Google doc, and paste the pertinent code into your text editor to try it out in your web browser (the full process for this is discussed shortly).

Accessing the book's referenced source code on the Google doc resource. Clicking on the HTML item in the Outline at screen left will bring you to the code associated with the book sections.

What This Book Assumes

In short, not much. This book assumes no prior knowledge of HTML or programming languages and presumes no prior experience with creating websites. The only thing assumed is that you have a computer to work on. By the end of this book, you will know how to create websites and structure the content on its pages using HTML5, and you will be well prepared for making deeper dives into the HTML specification and developer tools, and also moving on to learning CSS3, which is the coding language that stylizes HTML content. CSS3 is covered in the follow-on book to this one, *CSS3 Visual Learning Guide*.

Files and Directories

A website is just some files inside of folders, and the fancier computer science term for 'folder' is 'directory' so this will be our last use of the world 'folder!' On your computer you have files and directories and applications, so you are already familiar with the basic idea of what a website is and what its basic elements are, assuming you are familiar with computers. The main file types of websites are text files and media files. Text files contain the source code– such as HTML, CSS and JavaScript– and also textual content, such as titles, paragraphs, headings and articles. The media files may be comprised of images, audio, video, pdfs, zip files, executables, and other files that contain content beyond the textual content that is easily expressed in the source code, since the source code and text can easily coexist in a plain text file.

This is basically all a website is, files in directories (resist the urge to call directories folders).

There are many ways to organize files and directories. Above, we can say that the three files are text files with file extensions of **.html, .css** and **.js**. Regardless of the file extension used, they are all actually the same plain text file format. However, the web browser requires specialized coding language specific file extensions so that it knows how to parse the code and make websites out of them. So instead of the usual file extension **.txt** for text files, these text files are aimed at a browser and so take alternate file extensions that let a browser know what programming language is being used in them.

The media files will come from various places, and we won't worry too much about where they come from in this book. Photos and videos can come from your cell phone. Audio might come from downloaded sound effects libraries or Soundcloud accounts. PDFs can come from wherever you make PDFs. If you are a game designer, you might want people to download beta versions of your game as executables. If you are an accountant, you might have a client download a spreadsheet or their tax returns, and so on. All of these kinds of files are media rather than plain text files. Code lives in plain text files, since the code is just text and while it does amazing things, it doesn't require anything more than the kind of text that goes into any plain text **.txt** file. Code is just plain text, with file name extensions based on the language used in the text file so that the code can be executed. If you're coding in python, the file extension would be **.py**, or if you're coding in C++, it would be **.cpp**, etc. Regardless of these file name extensions, they are ALL just plain text of the **.txt** file extension type at heart (in fact, you could even save them as **.txt** files if you ever want to! There would be no real difference, except for what a browser can do with them).

The Other Tools

As mentioned above, you are already familiar with files, directories and applications from your everyday computer knowledge. We've covered the first two categories already. There are some applications you need to create a website, but these are generally free (though you can pay for some if you wish to boost the economy). The main applications you need are a web browser and a text editor. You need another application, called an FTP client, but since there are online browser-based FTP clients, technically these are already covered by browsers. However, you may also want to get a standalone FTP client application because some of the tool perks they can provide. An FTP client is what moves your files and directories from your computer where you organize them onto a web server so that it can go live on the web.

To develop your website skills, pick one of the mainstream browsers, such as Firefox or Chrome. You can go non-mainstream if you wish (Opera, anyone?). This book doesn't explore every browser variation there is. Whatever browser you select, make sure that you go into its settings and set the browser to automatically update itself, so that you always have the most recent version of your browser. This is important because hackers around the world are always looking for security flaws in software including browsers, and whenever a major security threat is identified, the browser code is updated but you won't get the update unless you remember to update it, or have the browser set to auto-update.

So the main applications you need to create websites are:

- code editor
- browser
- FTP client

You can design lots of websites with only the code editor and the browser, but then these websites will live only on your computer (we can still call these websites since they are viewable in a web browser). To get your website online, into the world wide web portion of the internet (there are other parts to the internet that we are not covering in this book), you will need access to a server. There are several options here, including:

- host your website on your own (or someone you know)'s web server
- pay a web hosting service their annual fee to host it for you
- explore search engine results under terms such as "free web hosting providers" and see what you find
- you may get free server space, e.g. if you are a student, or at work

Examples of popular ftp client applications are FileZilla, Cyberduck, Transmit, and SmartFTP, and Free FTP. Some FTP client applications, such as Transmit, have very simple drag and drop interfaces that let you simply drag the whole collection of files and directories from your desktop onto your server space. With some other FTP client applications you have to upload each file and create each directory manually. An example of an online FTP client is net2ftp.com. There are many to choose from and it doesn't matter for this book which option you go with.

The main pieces of information you need to know for using an FTP application are:

- your username
- your password
- the ftp server address

When you obtain the services of a web hosting service, you will obtain all of these as part of the process of signing on with them. If you have never uploaded a website to a server before, these hosting companies have help and chat lines where you can get assistance when you get stuck. Some web hosting services, free and paid for, include Bluehost, HostGator, HostPapa, GoDaddy, InterServer, Weebly, iPage, A2 Hosting, and Wix. Note that usually free website hosting services usually have a lot of restrictions attached, so do your comparisons and choose the one that makes sense for you.

When you login to your web hosting company's server, you will see a lot of other directories there and maybe some files. The directory you want to focus on is the one called pub_html. 'Pub' means 'public' and this will be the world-facing directory that you want to put your website files and directories in. You don't actually need to have a live website in order to work through all the examples this book, since you can see all of your code rendered on your personal computer in any browser. But you will need to figure out how to use an FTP client application eventually if you want to have a live world-facing website.

We should introduce a little more terminology here. The server is considered to be a 'backend' technology. It is 'behind the scenes' as it were. It serves up the website using technologies that are generally hidden from view (hidden from anyone who is not a backend developer or administrator, that is). The website as it lives in a browser facing a user and viewer is a 'frontend' technology, which is also referred to as 'client side' or 'client facing.' HTML5 is a front-end client-side technology. Back end technologies often include a full server stack of server tiers, where there may be three servers involved in a more complex web application– 1) the http server for delivering the website, 2) an application server for hosting software, and 3) another server dedicated solely to data. Here we are just presenting a little of the overall context technical of how a website gets stored and accessed, and we won't be going into the back end at all in this book. HTML and CSS are front end programming languages. JavaScript can be used either on the frontend or backend server side of the full technology stack. All the layers between frontend and backend are referred to collectively as 'the stack.'

To see your website design in a browser, all you have to do is save the code that you have typed in the text editor, name it `index.html`, and double click on it– the file will render in your default browser– that's all there is to it! You can name your page anything you like, but the home page is always called `index.html`. Always save .html files.

The last consideration here is the text editor (also called code editor). There are many to choose from. If you do a web search on "best code editors" or "best HTML editors", you will have many to choose from. Some come free but with upgraded versions you can pay for. For purposes of this book, the main things you are looking for in selecting one is syntax highlighting (so that different parts of the HTML syntax are colored categorically), auto-completion (meaning that when you create a code tag that is typically paired with another one, the paired element is created at the same time– this is just a convenience and not a necessity), a popup menu to quickly change the coding language to whatever you are typing in, auto-indentation to organize the lines neatly, and so on.

Note that not all code editors will use syntax highlighting in the same way or have all these tools in an easy-to-find way without needing some customization on your end. You'll have to explore the options and see which ones you like the best. It's not critical for the purposes of this book which tools you use, as they will all produce the same end result.

You can start with one code editor and always change to another later once you get the hang of what the features are. Some popular code editors include:

- `Sublime Text`
- `BBEdit`
- `Atom`
- `Brackets`
- `Visual Studio Code`

There are even online code editors like JSFiddle that allow you to type code online and see the results (JSFiddle allows you to type HTML, CSS and JavaScript in three different panels, and shows the results in a fourth panel when you run the code). A similar online code editor is Repl.it. Go to

```
https://repl.it/languages
```

and choose the language designation "HTML, CSS, JS: The languages that make up the web" and you can do all of your code editing in a browser! So, poke around on the internet and try out different code editors for writing your HTML. Once you find one that you want to use, use the following code as the starter template for all the websites you create as you work through this book:

```
<!DOCTYPE html>
<html>
<body>
</body>
</html>
```

Summary of Making .html Files

Here is the succinct summary of making HTML pages, just to reduce the preceding paragraphs into a few bullet points for fast reference:

- Open your chosen code editor (Sublime Text, Atom, Brackets, BBEdit, etc.)
- Set the syntax to HTML.
- Type your HTML into the document (or paste from this book's online code examples in the Google doc referred to earlier).
- Save the document with the .html extension.
- Open the saved document in your default browser by clicking on it.

If you want to live edit your code, modify the HTML in the code editor, save the file so the changes are reflected in the .html text file, then refresh your browser to see the changes you've made.

Alternately, you can use an online code editor like JSFiddle and do all of this in the browser and see the results when you click on 'RUN.'

Markup

Because websites are just files in directories, websites are also understood to be documents, and servers are thought of as storing and delivering documents when requested by users. HTTP, which you know from every web URL, stands for Hypertext Transfer Protocol, and what it transfers are documents (files in directories). HTML stands for Hypertext Markup Language. A markup language adds a hierarchical conceptual scheme to text-based content.

Here's an example– let's say I've written a really terrible song while bar hopping in Derry, Northern Ireland late one night. Such a terrible song might go like,

Awesome Song!

I am wandering around Derry
I had a lot of dark beer
The bands played lots of fiddles
I can't understand anyone's accent

- *by me!*

So, there we have the terrible song inspired by late night revelries. Now, let's add markup to it. Markup looks for high level conceptual categories that can be nested hierarchically to create a formal logic that ultimately is easy for browsers to parse, since browsers are all like *Star Trek's* Spock character, super logical.

So, let's create a markup for this terrible song. It won't be HTML markup but just illustrate a markup approach in general. We have a hierarchical and categorical scheme that might look like this:

```
<song>
      <title>Awesome Song!</title>
      <main_lyrics>
            <line1>I am wandering around Derry.</line1>
            <line2>I had a lot of dark beer.</line2>
            <line3>The bands played lots of
      fiddles.</line3>
            <line4>I can't understand anyone's
      accent.</line4>
      <main_lyrics>
      <author> - By Me!</author>
<song>
```

We are sneaking in a little HTML above, namely the <brackets> and the /forward slash. HTML uses opening and closing tags enclosed inside of brackets, and the difference between them is that the closing tag has a forward slash before the tag name. HTML opening and closing tags include:

```
<html></html>    //the whole html text file's content is
enclosed in these tags
<h1></h1>        //heading level one
<p></p>          //paragraph
<a></a>          //anchor, the HTML term for what we
normally call a link
```

I have to admit I'm sneaking in a little JavaScript above, too, since the two forward slashes, //, are used to create comments in JavaScript. A comment is text that is ignored by the code processor and is more intended to be a note to self, or a note to others, something that is useful to place in code– for example, to remember years later what it is you were trying to do when you wrote the code!

I used JavaScript comment syntax above, not to confuse you, but because one day you will have to learn JavaScript anyway and so you may as well get a little taste of it. Also, it's just much more succinct than the massive HTML comment syntax, which is written as   <!--   -->

Here's an example of an HTML comment.

```
<!-- omg we need all these extra characters to make a
comment in HTML, way more than JavaScript -- >
```

```
Here's a JavaScript comment:
```

```
//comment
```

We will keep JavaScript to a bare minimum in this book and focus of course on HTML5! But here and there a little Js (JavaScript's nickname) will creep in.

White spaces– that is, empty areas of text where there are no letters, but which have a presence in the code– can be tricky. Generally programming and markup languages ignore most white space but there are times where it's crucial for having the code execute properly. It will become clear in the examples used throughout this book when you do need to use white space, and when it doesn't matter. A lot of the conventions around the use of white spaces just have to do with readability, so that code is easier to parse by humans, versus machines. Some white space is recognized by HTML, because we obviously expect spaces between words. For example, look at this example of HTML-ignored white space shown below:

```
<!DOCTYPE html>
<html>
<body>
    <h1>A Big Heading</h1>
    <p>A normal paragraph.</p>
    <p>A      paragraph           with       lots of
    weird          white        space.          </p>
</body>
</html>
```

A Big Heading

A normal paragraph.

A paragraph with lots of weird white space.

HTML ignores a lot of white spaces

Note that some HTML tags are *empty* or *self-closing*, meaning they do not require a second tag with a forward slash before the tag name. In the example above, the DOCTYPE declaration is one of these self-closing tags, which is why you don't see a second one. Sometimes a self-closing tag will be full of added attributes and values before the final closing greater-than sign. Other times tags will be empty, as with the break **`<br>`** tag.

Also, HTML is not case sensitive. Good coding style conventions typically advise to type code in lower case or camelCase as it is easier to read. For example, the code below works fine even though the tags are expressed in ALL CAPS:

```
<!doctype html>
<HTML>
  <BODY>
    <H1>html does not care</H1>
    <P>about capitalization of tags</P>
  </BODY>
</HTML>
```

html does not care

about capitalization of tags

Stylistically gauche but still functional capitalized HTML tags

The Self-Closing Tags

Here is your handy list of all the tags that do not need a second closing version of itself with a forward slash added:

```
<area> <base> <br> <col> <command> <embed> <hr> <img>
<input> <keygen> <link> <meta> <param> <source> <track>
<wbr>
```

Note that you may sometimes come across examples online of these self-closing tags having a forward slash before the greater than sign, so you may see this instead:

```
<area/> <base/> <br/> <col/> <command/> <embed/> <hr/>
<img/> <input/> <keygen/> <link/> <meta/> <param/>
<source/> <track/> <wbr/>
```

These forward slashes at the end of a self-closing tag were used in previous versions of HTML. In HTML 5, you can omit them. Many browsers will continue to support this syntax, so that old websites will still render ok, since a certain amount of backwards compatibility is always desired so that websites can function well many years later after the browser technology has changed.

If you find it hard to remember which tags are self-closing, use a code editor that has autocompletion, like the online editor JSFiddle, which autocompletes HTML tags. If the autocompleting editor doesn't add the second closing tag, it is self-closing!

The Tree Structure (Parents and Children)

As you mark up your HTML documents, you will eventually start to indent a lot. In the template code above, nothing is indented because these are very high-level tags and so it saves you one indentation layer to ignore indentation at this level of the markup. Any HTML document will only have one **\<html\>** and one **\<body\>** tag, so there's no need to indent these. The tags are hierarchical in nature, meaning that they nest inside of each other in 'parent' and 'child' relationships. This nesting concept will become very clear as you go through the examples of the book– for now, just understand that it's a tree-like structure where one is either moving toward the top-most document node– the parent of all html elements– or away from it, which is in the direction of ever-more 'children' of the parents. The indentation syntax expresses this nesting parent-child tree structure, like so:

```
<!DOCTYPE html>
<html id="megaParent">
  <body id="childOfMegaParent">
    <div>
      <p id="justAParent">parent</p>
      <ul id="child">
        list of children
      </ul>
      <li
class="greatGreatGreatgrandchildOfMegaParent">child
1</li>
      <li
class="greatGreatGreatgrandchildOfMegaParent">child
2</li>
    </div>
  </body>
</html>
```

parent

list of children

- child 1
- child 2

Illustration of the hierarchical nesting of parent/child elements

The reason this is called a tree structure is because it can be modelled as a set of branches connected to each other, which can either be traced back to the main parent or follow all the branching lines of the children.

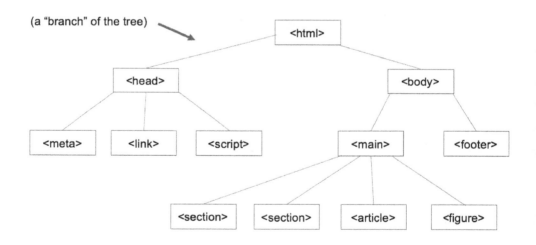

Markup as a tree structure.

The indentations in HTML code writing style are meant to be reflective of these parent/child, tree structure hierarchical relationships. There is no strong relationship between the HTML indentation and the final rendering of content on the screen. The tree structure of the HTML expresses a conceptual feature of HTML in that its tags exists in a hierarchical relationship to each other, which has important ramifications for the structure of the markup and what browsers do with it. The spatial rendering of content is something else entirely and indentation of HTML markup has little to do with content rendering on a screen.

Attributes and Values

In the HTML above, we saw additional writing inside of the tags, such as **id="..."** and **class="...."**. These are called *attributes* and they have *values* assigned to them via an = sign, and their values are indicated in quotes. Above, these **attribute="value"** pairs are somewhat whimsical as they are just being used to illustrate the parent/child hierarchy concept. Attributes and values are placed inside of tags to modify them in some way or give them some definitional specificity. Attributes come in two varieties, those that need a value expressed explicitly, and those which can stand alone as their own value. The syntax for these two types is:

```
<tag attribute="value">content</tag>

<tag attribute>content</tag>
```

id is an attribute that can be used for any HTML tag, and it supplies a unique identifier– a particular name that you give to it– as its value. In other words, ideally only one or very few HTML elements would share the same **id**. The **class** attribute is used when the same identifier needs to be assigned to a group of elements. These uses will become clearer in the following pages.

One use of ids and classes is to target styling instructions towards these specifically named elements, using either a . for a **class** or # for an **id**. Styling is the role of CSS (Cascading Style Sheets), which is discussed in the companion book to this one. In CSS, here is how you would target an **id** versus a **class**, for a paragraph (**<p>**) HTML element:

```
p.className {
    ...;
    }

p#idName {
    ...;
    }
```

You use attributes as you need to, for accomplishing specific goals. In other words, you do not have to use all of a tag's attributes, so just because the **<button>** tag, for instance, comes with eleven attributes, you need not use all eleven of them! The only attribute you should use with button elements is the **type** attribute (see the section later on the **<button>** tag for a fuller explanation. Attributes and their values will be well illustrated in the examples shown below, if these concepts are still a little hazy at this point.

As you go through the explanation of the tags, you might have a thought along the lines of, "Why are there so many granularly labelled ways to micro-label every last possible detail about HTML tags? For example, why do I need to give my button a **name** as an attribute that no one looking at the website can see?" The reason is because in the overall computational context, this 'hyper labelling activity' is needed to run scripts on the HTML document. There is a plethora of explanations as to why these techniques were developed. The reason one might name a button with an attribute that no one can see, is because JavaScript can see it. Code can seek out other code with these properties and values and do things with them. So that's the short answer! Only use the attributes needed to refine your particular use of a tag, and just know that millions of others are doing useful things with all the other attributes, tags and elements that you may never use.

Structure, Style, Interaction

The 'triumvirate' of coding languages used for the web is comprised of HTML, CSS and JavaScript. These are three languages you will ultimately need to become familiar and competent with. Each has its own syntax, because they each have different functions. Programming languages are different from each other because they do different things, addressing different contexts and operating at different levels of hardware, interface, display, content, communication, data and so on. HTML structures the content of a website. CSS styles it and gives control over the presentation of the HTML-structured content. JavaScript is a powerful general-purpose programming language which is used to create interactions and web applications, since a web browser can also be thought of as a ubiquitous software platform.

As HTML is presented in this book, we will constantly be bumping up against moments where a little CSS and JavaScript will creep into the discussion. For example, CSS styling can be added to an HTML document either with the `<style>` tag or `style=` as an attribute to an element. A number of HTML tags and attributes are directly tied to web applications, such as all those involved with creating forms and buttons, which feed directly to JavaScript. The `<canvas>` element provides a places in an HTML document for drawing images using JavaScript (sometimes referred to in this book just as 'Js'), and indeed there is an HTML tag `<script>` just for placing JavaScript directly into an HTML document. In these kinds of instances where we cannot avoid talking about Js and CSS, we will cover just the minimum amount of context needed to understand what HTML is doing at these places of direct interface with these other coding languages.

Tags vs Elements

So far, I have been using the terms 'tag' and 'element' in a way that may seem interchangeable, but they are not exactly so. The tag is the html object that is enclosed in the arrow brackets. These are examples of tags:

```
<p>
<article>
<title>
<head>
<footer>
```

An element is the complete expression of a tag with its content, and perhaps as modified by additional **attribute="value"** pairs. Here is a basic HTML element with just content and its tags:

```
<p>I need coffee.</p>
```

This is the paragraph *tag* (**<p>**) enclosing the content "I need coffee." This whole construction is an HTML *element*.

However, to make matters perhaps a bit more confusing, the HTML5 Standard does refer to the tags as elements, e.g. it will refer to the concept of an *element* when discussing the properties and attributes, use cases etc. of the various HTML tags. In this book, we will tend to refer to *tags* directly as what is enclosed with the arrow brackets and use the term element for more complete expressions which include content and any **attribute="value"** pairs modifying them. So **<title>** is a tag, in this book's usage, while **<title>The Book's Title</title>** is an element.

Styling

Let's say that we want the color of this sentence about coffee to render in red. We might code this as:

```
<!DOCTYPE html>
<html>
  <body>
    <p style="color:red">I need red coffee!</p>
  </body>
</html>
```

I need red coffee!
Making coffee red, without Red Bull.

The whole construction of `<p style="color:red">I need coffee.</p>` is also an *element*, it is just a more complicated one, because it is doing more work. In HTML, `<style>` is also a tag unto itself, but in this context, it is being used as an *attribute* of the `<p>` (paragraph) tag, meaning that it is modifying the standard visual presentation in some way. This particular attribute as shown here has two components, a *property* (color), and a value (red). So sometimes instead of the construction **attribute="value"** inside of the opening HTML tag, we instead have a construction of **attribute="property:value."** This is especially the case when using CSS because it is largely based on **property:value** pairs, which themselves become nested into the value of a style attribute within an HTML tag.

It is worth mentioning that this is more or less the same (but somewhat re-arranged) syntax as we find in CSS3. In CSS, an HTML tag is called a **selector** and the **property:value** pairings are also expressed within **{curly braces}**, have colons connecting them, and are completed with semicolons.

As we do with HTML's **style** attribute, if we want to daisy chain multiple stylings to an element, we separate them with a semicolon. The overall syntax of CSS looks like this:

```
selector {
     property:value;
     property:value;
     }
```

So, if we also want to center-align our red coffee text, we would write:

```
<p style="color:red; text-align:center">I need
coffee.</p>
```

In CSS, this would be written as

```
p {
     color:red;
```

```
      text-align:center;
}
```

As you can see, this styling syntax is basically the same, it's just rearranged a bit in the different contexts of CSS and HTML. Note that in CSS, it's considered good code writing style to add a semicolon after the final **property:value** pairing, whereas in HTML the final pairing can omit the semicolon.

In this book, we will mostly use what is called inline CSS, because our focus is on HTML and so we want to keep HTML tags and elements as the core focus. Inline CSS is when you write your styling information within an HTML tag, using the **style** attribute followed by the **property:value** pairing(s) in quotation marks. There are two other ways to use CSS in HTML documents: as a link to an external text file, and as an internal style sheet.

The CSS companion book mostly uses external stylesheets as the focus, in contrast to the inline CSS used in this book. Here, as we cover HTML5, we are not going to style our content that much, just a bit here and there to teach the core concepts. The standard way of styling websites is to link to external CSS scripts that are located in other text (.css) files on the web server. We will discuss this more when we come to the **<script>** tag later in this book.

The third way of using CSS is via what is called "Internal CSS" to basically write a bit of CSS syntax within the HTML document, in the **<head>** section and by using the **<style>** tag. Internal CSS looks like this:

```
<!DOCTYPE html>
<html>
  <head>
    <style type=text/css>
        h1 {color: red;}
        p {color: black;}
    </style>
  </head>
  <body>
```

```
    <h1>Red Heading Not Herring</h1>
    <p>Black coffee is fine, too.</p>
  </body>
</html>
```

Red Heading, Not Herring

Black coffee is fine, too.

Internal CSS, in the `<head>` *section of an HTML document expressed within* `<style>` *tags.*

In this book we will mostly not be using internal CSS, but it does need to be mentioned because it is one of the three ways to include CSS styling in an HTML document. A good use case for internal CSS is when you have a single page website with minimal styling requirements. All code, whether in markup or a general-purpose programming language such as JavaScript or C++, processes the code in a linear, top to bottom fashion. What comes first is processed first, and this of course has major ramifications on the results. Internal CSS is placed at the top, in the **<head>** section, before the elements in the **<body>** section, because we want the browser to parse the styling first before it renders the content.

If we didn't do it this way, and put internal CSS at the bottom instead, the content would first be presented as plain ol' (somewhat ugly, nonstyled) HTML, and then, after the page has loaded as a rather raw-looking HTML document, apply the style at the end of the page load–obviously this makes no sense. We want to browser instead to understand the stylistic requirements before presenting the content, and so internal CSS goes in the **<head>** section (as do other elements we want to be parsed first before the subsequent elements in the **<body>** section).

Special Characters

There are a number of special characters that have unique identifiers for them, which should be used in the .html file to assure that they render correctly in the browser. Here are some examples of special characters, and the HTML codes that represent them:

```
&        &amp;
£        &pound;
®        &reg;
½        &frac12;
⇔        &hArr;
```

Special characters can be expressed in either Number Codes or Entity Codes. For the full list, visit `http://bit.ly/specChar`

Semantic Tags

Some tags in HTML5 have a semantic meaning that we can obtain just by reading them which relate to the kinds of content they enclose, whereas other tags lack this semantic quality. The `<div>` tag, for instance, only specifies a general spatial container or 'division' of the HTML page and so names a place where some kind of content can be placed. However, `<div>` says nothing directly about the *kinds of content* that may be associated with it.

Many tags also divide the page into sections but also convey content aspects through the semantics of the tag name itself. Examples of these semantic tags are **`<article>`, `<figure>`, `<blockquote>`** and **`<aside>`.** In general you should aim to use semantically meaningful tags whenever possible, as this helps both with automated machine reading of site content, and also with accessibility devices and settings. You can tell which tags are semantic if they convey a clear meaning about the kinds of content they may contain, since semantic tags have an everyday meaning to them. In everyday language, no one knows what a *div* is, but everyone knows what a *video* is. Use semantic tags as often as possible to create clearer human and machine-readable code.

Name Things Well

When you assign your own names to the values inside of elements via their attribute assignments, avoid special characters and white spaces, don't start your label with a number, and use lowercase or camelCase as much as possible to stay out of syntactical trouble. Camel case:

```
looksLikeThis
whereYouStartLowercase
andCombineWordsWithFirstLetter
capitalizedLikeShownHere
```

Try to stick to straightforward easy-to-understand unique names that you add into the HTML, so that your future self, or others looking at the same code, can grasp quickly what is intended by your original labelling schemes.

Block and Inline Display Properties

As one combines multiple HTML tags to structure a document, they will either be displayed horizontally in a line without line breaks– which is called *inline* display– or they will stack vertically above each other, which is called *block* display. These display types are defaults and can be overridden through explicit styling instructions, so one can make inline elements display on a page as though they were block elements, and vice versa. To make block tags display as inline elements, use **inline-block** as the declared display value. Below we show how similar elements can display differently based on using either their default or modified display type.

```
<!DOCTYPE html>
<html>
  <body>
    <div style="background-color:pink;">
      <h1 style="padding: 10px;">Heading Number 1</h1>
      <p style="padding: 10px;">Paragraph Number 1</p>
    </div>
    <div style="background-color:cyan;">
      <h1 style="padding: 10px;">Heading Number 2</h1>
      <p style="padding: 10px;">Paragraph Number 2</p>
    </div>
    <div style="background-color:pink; display: inline-
block;">
      <h1 style="padding: 10px;">Heading Number 3</h1>
      <p style="padding: 10px;">Paragraph Number 3</p>
    </div>
    <div style="background-color:cyan; display: inline-
block;">
      <h1 style="padding: 10px;">Heading Number 4</h1>
      <p style="padding: 10px;">Paragraph Number 4</p>
    </div>
  </body>
</html>
```

Heading Number 1

Paragraph Number 1

Heading Number 2

Paragraph Number 2

Heading Number 3   Heading Number 4

Paragraph Number 3   Paragraph Number 4

Styling `<div>` elements to display either as default block or modified inline via the `inline-block` display value

Below are lists of HTML tags organized by whether they display as block or inline by default.

Block display by default tags

```
<address>
<article>
<aside>
<blockquote>
<canvas>
<dd>
<div>
<dl>
<dt>
<fieldset>
<figcaption>
<figure>
<footer>
<form>
```

```
<h1-h6>
<header>
<hr>
<li>
<main>
<nav>
<noscript>
<ol>
<p>
<pre>
<section>
<table>
<tfoot>
<ul>
<video>
```

Inline display by default tags

```
<a>
<abbr>
<acronym>
<b>
<bdo>
<big>
<br>
<button>
<cite>
<code>
<dfn>
<em>
<i>
<img>
<input>
<kbd>
<label>
<map>
<object>
<output>
<q>
<samp>
```

```
<script>
<select>
<small>
<span>
<strong>
<sub>
<sup>
<textarea>
<time>
<tt>
<var>
```

Note that some of the tags listed above date from earlier versions of HTML and are no longer part of the HTML5 specification, so you will not see some of these tags (such as **`<acronym>`** discussed in this book.

Hopefully you have already been reading in the most active manner possible, by actually trying out these HTML examples in your chosen code editor, saving .html files, and opening them up in your browser to see how they render. We are now ready to dive in! The rest of the book is devoted to illustrating concretely and visually all the HTML tags, making elements out of them and customizing them with attributes and values. While the book cannot cover all of their infinite combinations, in a clear and concise manner these pages will aim to get you inspired and feeling confident to create your own websites from scratch using your new coding skills.

Bit.ly URL Shortener Note

Peppered throughout this book are shortened URLs with a small number of semantically useful characters for quickly typing into your browser. These custom links support quick access to more copious online resources than are possible to summarize in this book. These URLs will always begin with `http://bit.ly/` and there is a full list of all `bit.ly` links at the end of the book.

The Tags & Elements

Now we will explore the HTML tags, mostly in alphabetical order, and give examples of their display in a browser as they are used to construct complete elements and structure the content of an HTML document. As you read through the descriptions, try out the examples in your text editor by pasting them over from the Google doc mentioned in the Introduction, save the .html file, and open it in your browser by double clicking on it to see the results.

<!-- -->

If you want to leave the equivalent of "notes to self" in your code, and not have it displayed in the browser (unless the viewer right-clicks on the page and chooses View Source), then use the comment tag to wrap your thoughts which will not be displayed. The browser will ignore rendering or processing anything in these tags.

Another use for comments is to temporarily disable lines of code to see the effect on the rendering of the page in the browser. You can wrap your HTML code in the comment tags, hit refresh on the browser (after saving your file of course) and the page will display as though the code lines were absent. You can bring the code back to functionality by deleting the comment tags.

```
<!-- This text will not render on the screen -->
<p>But this text will!</p>
```

<!DOCTYPE html>

Every `.html` text file has to begin with this declaration, which lets the browser know that this begins an HTML page. **<!DOCTYPE html>** comes before the **<html>** tag. **<!DOCTYPE html>** is technically not an HTML tag, but rather an instruction given to the browser about the version of HTML being used. Older versions of HTML required more information than this simple form of the declaration. For example, in HTML4 you would see this declaration at the top of the text file:

```
<!DOCTYPE HTML PUBLIC "-//W3C//DTD HTML 4.01
Frameset//EN" "http://www.w3.org/TR/html4/frameset.dtd">
```

If you use the View Source feature (or alternately, the Inspect feature) in the browser developer tools, which is accessed by right-clicking on any web page, you will often see earlier styles of writing HTML being used if the code hasn't been updated in awhile, so it's worth knowing that older versions of HTML used different conventions.

\<a\>

This tag is for hyperlinks and stands for 'anchor.' In some WYSIWYG editors (this stands for "what you see is what you get" and has an interface that looks more like a word processor than a code editor), **\<a\>** tags are sometimes depicted as little anchor icons. This is because when the tag was originally created, it was used for linking to items within the same electronic document, rather than jumping out to other documents as we are accustomed to doing today. In the early days of the web, one might link a table of contents line to a later section of the text, or link to a footnote in an article, all of which were operations in the same document, and so the idea of an "anchor" made more sense. Today we mostly use hyperlinks more like teleportation devices to jump to web content located somewhere else on a server far, far away, with the main exception being single page scroller websites where we do use **\<a\>** elements more like the original function to change sections by scrolling to them. Anchors can be used to link to many kinds of resources, such as email addresses, file downloads, and other content elsewhere on the same page.

Hyperlink Default Styling

There is some default styling applied to hyperlinks. Without adding any explicit styling in your code to overrule these defaults, unvisited links will be underlined in blue, links will turn purple and stay underlined when visited, and a link that is active is red and underlined. You can change these defaults by adding new style information.

`<a>` Attributes

The main attribute is **href**, which specifies what one is linking *to*. This can be either an absolute or a relative link. An absolute link will have a URL address as the content beginning with `http://` or `https://` (the second version is the more secure version of the same URL), whereas a relative link will specify the path to be followed from the page's location in the browser directory to the file it is referencing. If the relative path begins with a forward slash / it will indicate a directory within the same directory where the `.html` file is located. If there is no forward slash / then the file would have to be in the same folder as the `.html` document.

Let's illustrate the difference between relative and absolute URLs as a value to the **href** attribute. Below, we show the results of having created a website in a sloppy manner, where we have left a PDF all by itself in the same directory as the **index.html** file, instead of placing it in a directory called "assets" or some other well-named directory, in the same way that scripts and images have their own directories as shown here:

index.html

pdf.pdf

scripts

images

Sloppy file and directory structure for illustration purposes.

Even though this is sloppy organization, we can still produce the correct code to allow a user to download the pdf in spite of our sloppiness. If we wanted to place a link in the document so that a site visitor can download the PDF, the html might look like this:

```
<p><a href="pdf.pdf">Download your pdf!</a></p>
```

In this instance, the **href** attribute's value need only be the name of the PDF file, since it is in the same directory as the `index.html` file. If someone pointed out how sloppy or coding was, and instructed us to create an assets directory, alongside scripts and images, then our html would be written like this, using a forward slash to navigate to the directory where the file is located:

```
<p><a href="assets/pdf.pdf">Download your pdf!</a></p>
```

This is because the assets folder would be in the same directory as the `index.html` file, and we access the contents of that directory with the forward slash. If there was a PDF inside of a directory called "pdf" which was nested inside of the assets folder, the html would like this instead:

```
<p><a href="assets/pdf/pdf.pdf">Download your
pdf!</a></p>
```

If you run into any issues making your paths work, double check spelling, letter case and file extensions. E.g. don't call your photo "photo.jpeg" in the html if is actually called "photo.jpg" in the directory! If you are linking to a live website, just enter the full web address as the value to the **href** attribute beginning with "http://...".

If the link is to explicitly download content, adding the attribute **download** after the path name will direct the browser to download the file (as opposed to, for instance, just opening it up in the browser, which will in part also depend on the type of file that is being referenced for download). Download can also take an optional property of naming the document to be downloaded.

The **hreflang** attribute is an attribute that explicitly names the language of the document being linked to. HTML documents referencing different languages typically use ISO 639-1 language codes in which dozens of languages are coded in two-letter formats. You can see the full list at:

```
http://bit.ly/ISOlangCode
```

Here are some examples:

```
Basque = eu
English = en
Greek = el
Haitian Creole = ht
Javanese = jv
```

The **media** attribute (which can be used if an **href** is present) tells the browser what target device the site has been designed for, in order to produce an optimal experience. For example, **media="all"** would mean that the content renders well on all displays and devices. Specifications for multiple devices can be used by using these logical operators:

- and

- not

- , (note: a comma is used as the logical operator that means 'or').

The device values that can be used as values for the media attribute include speech synthesizers (**aural**), braille devices (**braille**), small handhelds (**handheld**), projectors (**projection**), print for pages and preview (**print**), screens (**screen**), teletypes (**tty**) and lower resolution televisions (**tv**). The terms inside the parentheses are the values taken by the media attribute, which hopefully is starting to become clearer.

In addition to these device specifications, there are additional `property:value` pairs that add more granularity as to what is possible to target in terms of display sizes and quality. You might add these additional pairings to the specified device with one of the logical operators. For example, a larger display could be targeted with the media attribute:

```
media="screen and (min-width: 1400px)"
```

This `attribute:value` pairing is looking for a screen that is at least (mid-width) 1400px wide.

The additional properties that are used for doing more fine-tuned media targeting are:

```
aspect-ratio
color
color-index
device-aspect-ratio
device-height
device-width
grid
height
monochrome
orientation
scan
width
```

The **ping** attribute can be used to send an HTML POST request to a designated web server if the link is clicked on. This provides one way of tracking user behavior on a site, so that if the link is clicked, the site creator is notified. HTML POST requests are a type of behavior one finds in other HTML tags, such as when a form has been filled out and the data is sent along to its destination. It relates to a more back end server-side topic which is out of scope for this book.

The **rel** attribute in this context specifies the nature of the *relationship* between the document with the link and the resource being linked to. The possible relationships (which are values to the **rel** attribute) that can be named between the link and its resource are:

- **alternate** gives an alternate URL for the link.

- **author** gives a link to the author of the page.

- **bookmark** is used for creating bookmarks.

- **external** indicates that the link is to some other website.

- **help** indicates that the link is to a help resource.

- **license** provides a link to a licensing reference.

- **next** links to the next document if it is part of a sequence of pages.

- **nofollow** asks web spiders not to follow you as you on the web as you activate the link.

- **noreferrer** asks the browser not to send HTTP referrer information.

- **noopener** is a security value that requires the next page not to have any window openers active, which might exploit a vulnerability.

- **prev** specifies a link to a web page that is the previous one in a sequence.

- **search** indicates a link to a search feature.

- **tag** gives a keywords for the web page.

When you are first starting to create websites, most of these rel values are not necessary to use. If you would like to see an in-depth discussion on each of these, refer to `http://bit.ly/linkATTR`

Along with **href**, **target** is one of the most used attributes on **<a>** tags, as it specifies how the link should be opened in the browser. For instance, typically one either opens a web page in the same browser window (which takes the value **"_self"**), or a new browser tab (which takes the value **"_blank"**). The values for target are:

_blank   opens the page in a new tab.
_parent   opens the page in the parent browsing context.
_self opens the page in the current browser frame.
_top   the top-most context for browsing.

The **type** attribute is used to designate what are called Media Types (which used to be called MIME types). A typical use is to describe the kind of text file being linked to. For instance, when linking to a stylesheet one will designate the media type as:

`type="text/css"`

There are hundreds of possible media types one can link to, for the full list, visit `http://bit.ly/mediaTypes`.

Here is an example of some HTML defining links.

```
<!DOCTYPE html>
<html>
  <body>
    <a href="http://...etc...">Link to this outside web
page!</a><br>
    <a href="/images/image">Link to this image on the
same server as this web page.</a><br>
    <a href="/images/image" media="braille and
handheld">This content renders best on Braille and
handheld devices</a><br>
```

```
    <a href="/images/image" media="braille and (min-
resolution: 326px)">Links to 8K high res video.</a><br>
    <a href="/CSS/css.css" type="text/css)">Links to a
CSS text file.</a><br>
    <a href="http://...etc..." hreflang="af">Link to this
web page in Afrikaans.</a><br>
    <a href="/directory/someFileToDownload"
download>Download this!</a><br>
    <a href="/directory/someFileToDownload"
download="downloadThis">Download this explicitly named
file!</a><br>
    <a href="a url..." ping="another url">Notify a
website if a user clicks on the link.</a><br>
    <a href="a url..." rel="help" target="_blank">This is
a very helpful help link in a new tab.</a><br>
  </body>
</html>
```

Link to this outside web page!

Link to this image on the same server as this web page.

This content renders best on Braille and handheld devices.

Links to 8K high res video.

Links to a CSS text file.

Link to this web page in Afrikaans.

Download this!

Download this explicitly named file!

Notify a website if a user clicks on this link.

This is a very helpful link in a new tab.

The <a> tag code as rendered.

In the code above, note that in order to get the hyperlinks to display vertically, we used the **
** (break) tag at the end of each element to display each link on a new line by breaking them off from the previous line. **<a>** tags by default display to *inline* style, meaning that by default they will display on the screen horizontally left to right unless made to behave otherwise. Here, we override this default behavior by adding **
** (or break, discussed shortly) to get the links to display vertically in block display style.

Navigation on the Same Page with ID

An **id** attribute can also be used to provide the ability to hop or bop around within a document, where an anchor can take the user to another section of the same page. Many websites are long scrollers where the navigation links simply move your view up and down the same page a lot, which economizes on the user experience by avoiding the time it takes to load additional pages. For example, let's say we had an author's web page and a link towards the top directing us to check out the author's bio, which is at the bottom of the page, beneath their photo and some paragraphs about them and their book covers etc. The **href** attribute to an anchor would use the hashtag **#** to indicate the **id** of the HTML element the page will go to when clicked on, and might look something like this:

```
<a href="#authorBio">Read the author's bio.</a>
<!-- ……(more lines of code)
……(author's head shot, book covers, critical praise,
etc.) -->
<p><a id="authorBio">Author Bio</a></p>
```

\<abbr\>

The **\<abbr\>** tag is used for defining acronyms or abbreviations. This tag can be helpful for the machine reading of websites, so that scripts get at the meaning inside of letters that form an abbreviation. In this way, for instance, a browser can understand the difference between POW (a 'prisoner of war') and the comic book punching sound, Pow! The full meaning of the text that is abbreviated is provided as the text value to the global **title** attribute, which plays a particular role with **\<abbr\>** tags.

```
<!DOCTYPE html>
<html>
  <body>
    <p>The controversy around <abbr title="North American
Free Trade Agreement">NAFTA</abbr> never seems to go
away</p>
  </body>
</html>
```

Abbreviations display the full name when a user mouses over the text.

<address>

The **<address>** tag designates contact information for the content of its nearest parent element. If placed inside of the **<article>** tag, it represents the author of the article, while if it is located in the **<body>** tag, it refers to the contact information of the whole document. Addresses will usually render by default in italics. Also, a **mailto:** value to an **href** attribute might also be included, if an email link is embedded in the element. An address element can take any kind of contact information, including phone, spatial coordinates, and social media profiles.

```
<!DOCTYPE html>
<html>
  <body>
    <address>
      Reach out to the owner-author at (social media
link)<br>
      Email <a href="mailto:email@address.com">Owner
Author's Name</a>
      Street Address<br>
      City, State and Postal<br>
      Country<br>
    </address>
  </body>
</html>
```

Reach out to the owner-author at (social media link)
Email Owner Author's Name Street Address
City, State and Postal
Country

Usage of the <address> *tag.*

<area>

The **<area>** tag is used inside of a **<map>** tag to create clickable areas known as 'hotspots' inside of an image. When we click on these areas, we activate a link that produces some kind of change in the browser. This would allow switching to a new photo which has some other kind of relationship to the original mapped photo. To give another example, if the website is an interactive detective fiction, clicking on an object in an image might take us to a popup clue file for solving the case. Let's look at some sample **<area>** code:

```
<!DOCTYPE html>
<html>
  <body>
    <img src="http://bit.ly/33y4EuS" width="300"
height="300" alt="city" usemap="#city">
    <map name="city">
      <area shape="rect" coords="0,0,300,100"
href="clouds.htm" alt="sky">
      <area shape="rect" coords="0,101,300,200"
href="buildings.htm" alt="buildings">
      <area shape="rect" coords="0,201,300,300"
href="street.htm" alt="ground">
    </map>
  </body>
</html>
```

<area> *code and its associated image reference.*

Because of the relative complexity of making areas of image clickable, we will talk briefly about the **<img>** and **<map>** tags (discussed in more detail below) and their respective attributes, **alt**, and **name**. The **<img>** and **<area>** tags are both self-closing, so you will note that these tags are somewhat complete in themselves without needing a second closing tag with a forward slash /. The **src** attribute of the image specifies where the image is located, which could be either an internal relative link– meaning, the image is in a directory on the same server as the website– or an absolute link to an image live on the web. Here, we are using an open access image that is live on the web and accessing it via its url (one finds an image's URL by right clicking on it and selecting "copy image address" as the direct link to it, which makes it usable).

To make it easy for illustrating clickable zones in the image defined by **<img>**, we have made the image into a pure square, with **width** and **height** attributes each set to 300 pixels (referred to as **px**). The **alt** attribute gives an alternative name for the image, which is used be accessibility devices. For instance, if the site is being accessed in a Braille reader, the value stored in **alt** makes the content accessible to impaired users, similar to subtitles for closed captioning of sound and dialogue in audio-visual media. The attribute **usemap** tells the browser that the image is to be parsed as a map for clickable areas, and it has to be given a specific name, starting with a hashtag, that will be referenced (sans hashtag!) by the **name** attribute of **<map>**.

To create clickable zones in a web-based image enclosed in the **<img>** tag, you should understand the coordinate system to be used. Whereas **X,Y coordinates** in trigonometry and other mathematical fields place the **0,0** origin at the center of a 2D matrix, in computer graphics the convention is usually to place the **0,0** origin at the top left corner, as shown below.

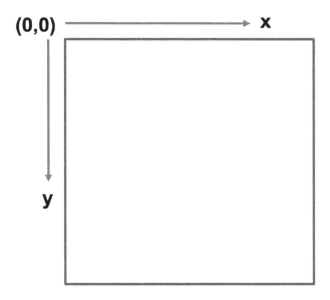

The X,Y coordinate system used in many computer graphics contexts.

When creating clickable areas on an image, the choices for the area to overlay onto the image are rectangles (**rect**), **circle**, polygon (**poly**) – which can be any shape with straight edges– and **default**, which covers the entire image. In the example above, we have carved the image up into three zones– upper, middle and bottom bands of 100 pixels in height each roughly corresponding to the sky (upper third), buildings (middle band) and road (bottom third). The coordinates one enters for each zone work as follows:

For rectangles, the first two numbers are the X,Y pair for the top left corner, and the second pair of numbers indicate the bottom right corner.

For circles, one specifies the X,Y coordinate of the center, and also the radius.

For polygons, one specifies all the vertices which define each edge. If the last vertex doesn't close the polygon shape, the browser will join automatically the last to the first vertice.

Each shape overlaid onto an image as a clickable zone also gets its own **href** attribute and **alt** name value. One way to know if your code is rendering correctly in the browser is to hover the mouse over the intended target. If area of the image is clickable, the cursor will change to the pointing finger variety, indicating that there's a link present. You can comment out each zone as you define them, to make sure that the cursor change is happening where you want it to. For example, below two **<area>** elements have been turned into comments– which are ignored by the browser– for verifying that the bottom third clickable area is positioned correctly in the image by watching the cursor change to a pointy finger:

```
<!-- <area shape="rect" coords="0,0,300,100"
href="clouds.htm" alt="sky">
<area shape="rect" coords="0,101,300,200"
href="buildings.htm" alt="buildings"> -->
<area shape="rect" coords="0,201,300,300"
href="street.htm" alt="ground">
```

The `<area>` tag has attributes that we've seen already: **alt, href, hreflang, media, rel** (though with a different set of values pertinent to area tags), **target,** and **type.**

`<article>`

The article tag is used for areas of self-contained content that hypothetically could be distributed on their own separately from the rest of the website. Examples of content that might be enclosed by `<article>` include forum or blog posts, news articles and comments. An HTML document might have many `<article>`s in the same way it could have multiple `<section>`s and other content container types . Articles usually take identifying headings or titles of some kind, and often contain publishing dates as well.

```
<!DOCTYPE html>
<html>

  <body>
    <article>Blog Post #1</article>
    <article>Blog Post #2</article>
    <article>Blog Post #1</article>
    <article>Recipe #1</article>
    <article>Recipe #2</article>
    <article>Recipe #1</article>
  </body>
</html>
```

`<aside>`

An aside is content related to but separated from some other content it is associated with. For example, information in a paragraph or article might be highlighted for additional emphasis, such as with a sidebar, is an aside. It is a semantic content container which specifies its particular role in the overall context of the page.

<audio>

```
<!DOCTYPE html>
<html>

<body>
  <audio controls>
    <source src="sound.ogg" type="audio/ogg">
    <source src="sound.mp3" type="audio/mpeg">
  </audio>
</body>
</html>
```

Audio content with controls for playback specified in the code.

The **<audio>** tag is for playing audio content in the browser. Audio files on the web are usually compressed for more efficient playback, since smaller files will stream more quickly than larger files. When including audio content on a website, multiple copies of the same audio file are referenced– each copy using a different compression format– since not all audio formats are supported by all browsers.

Audio files should be included, using the self-closing **<source>** tags, using mp3, ogg and wav codecs since these are supported by **<audio>**. The browser will select the best file to play as it goes down the list of options in the code. The **<source>** attribute **type** takes one of the three Media Types: **audio/mpeg, audio/ogg,** or **audio/wav. <audio>** has the following attribute and value options:

- **autoplay** will set the audio to play when it has been loaded into the browser.

- **controls** will show the controller information (depicted above).

- **loop** will set the audio to play a loop, repeating every time it finishes.

- **muted** will mute the audio output, perhaps to be unmuted later through JavaScript interactions.

- **preload** has three possible value settings: **auto, metadata,** and **none.** These values are for shaping the overall user experience.

- **auto** is used for loading the entire audio file when the page loads.

- **metadata** loads only the metadata associated with the audio file when the page loads.

- **none** instructs the browser *not* to load the audio file on page load.

- **src** gives the URL source information for locating the sound file.

<b>

This is the bold tag, currently known as the "bring attention to" tag since CSS has the **font-weight** property to make text bold. In HTML5, something which might seem very simple, like making text bold, is actually a somewhat granular affair! The 'issue' with bold as a tag concept is that it has no semantic meaning. Just as a **<div>** tag simply carves up content space on an html document without declaring why it's doing what it's doing through its tag name, bold is similar in that it simply declares that some text shall have a bold font weight value without indicating why it has been so emboldened.

<b> is often considered to be a "last resort" use case in HTML5. The HTML specification says to use the heading tags, **<h1>** to **<h6>** (discussed below) for all headings. Text that should be understood as being emphasized should use the **<em>** tag. Important content should use the **<strong>** tag, and text that is supposed to be understood as having been highlighted should use **<mark>**. So if you are tempted to just use **<b>** to make text bold, drill down a bit into your reasons why and see if any of the other tags on offer make more sense, so that your coding style will partake in HTML5 semantic conventions.

<base>

The base tag is placed in the **<head>** to describe a root URL, relative to which subsequent URLs placed as values to **href** attributes will read like relative paths. For example, if this were our code...

```
<!DOCTYPE html>
<html>
     <head>
        <base href="http://yourMainWebsite.com"
target="_blank">
     </head>
     <body>
       <img src="images/image.jpg">
     </body>
```

```
</html>
```

...then the actual full URL for the **img src** would be:

```
http://yourMainWebsite.com/images/image.jpg
```

Note that **<base>**, like **<img>,** is a self-closing tag. The base tag is useful if you are going to be drawing a lot of your media resources from a single URL (instead of from multiple URL sources) and so you might benefit from this kind of shorthand approach to all subsequent (post-base) **href** URLs. There can only be one base tag on an HTML document, because of the way the other URLs build on it.

Base takes the attributes **href** and **target.**

<bdi>

This tag's name stands for "bi-directional isolation" and provides a way for treating text that might be inserted dynamically, by JavaScript, into an HTML document which might be written in a different direction. Such insertions might involve the use of other languages such as Arabic, that are read right-to-left instead of left-to-right, as in Western languages. The **<bdi>** tag is wrapped around whatever text might be inserted into the surrounding text in a different reading direction. For instance:

```
<p>This user's name is <bdi>....<.bdi>rest of the
sentence.</p>
```

Here, the ellipses ... allows for insertion of names that may be entered in either directional mode, which might be useful if one is expecting international users where different kinds of writing directions may show up.

<bdo>

The bidirectional override tag allows you to override the default language direction by selecting either the right-to-left (**rtl**) or left-to-right (**ltr**) values to its **dir** (direction) attribute.

```
<!DOCTYPE html>
<html>
  <body>
    <p>
      OK so here is a paragraph written in the usual
English direction, and now...
    </p>
    <bdo dir="rtl">
      OK so here is a paragraph written in the usual
English direction, and now...
    </bdo>
  </body>
</html>
```

OK so here is a paragraph written in the usual English direction, and now...

hsilgnE lausu eht ni nettirw hpargarap a si ereh os KO
...won dna ,noitcerid

This is how you can make text be written backwards in HTML.

Aside from just making text go backwards, it provides a way to format text from languages that are written in the opposite direction from the surrounding context.

<blockquote>

Blockquotes are used to cite longer passages from other sources which are named explicitly as a URL value (either a relative path or absolute http address) to its **cite** attribute. As a styling note, longer passages of quoted text are typically indented within in the overall page layout. These indentations can be done with CSS properties such as **margin-left** or **margin-right**.

```
<!DOCTYPE html>
<html>
<body>
     <blockquote
cite="http://www.someOnlineBigEncyclopedia/index.html">
          The periodic chart predicts the appearance of
          yet-to-be-discovered heavy elements which must
          be the logical fuel source of alien spacecraft
          with antigravity drives and antimatter
          reactors.
     </blockquote>
</body>
</html>
```

<body>

The body tag encompasses most of the content of a website– this is where the text, headings, images, videos, charts, downloads and even some should scripts go. It is one of the highest-level parent elements in HTML, since its only parent is the **<html>** tag itself. It has no attributes, though older versions of HTML did have some which you might see on old websites, such as **alink, background, text, vlink** etc. which had to do with its layout, but which are no longer a part of the HTML5 standard. If you see body attributes you should know that it is from older code standards. There can only be one **<body>** per HTML document.

\

The break tag starts a new line and is often used to display content in a block rather than inline fashion, since it sets the follow-on elements below it. It is sometimes referred to as the 'carriage return' in reference to old typewriter terminology. For example, below we see three buttons, which while coded vertically in the HTML document, actually render on the screen horizontally because they are by default inline display elements.

```
<button type= "submit">Chocolate</button>
<button type= "submit">Strawberry</button>
<button type= "submit">Vanilla</button>
```

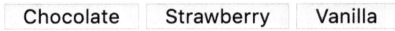

*As noted in the Introduction, **\<button>** by default displays in a horizontal or inline style.*

If we want to stack our buttons vertically, an easy way to do this is to add a **\
** tag after each button like so, since each break tag starts a new line:

```
<button type= "submit">Chocolate</button><br>
<button type= "submit">Strawberry</button><br>
<button type= "submit">Vanilla</button><br>
```

> Chocolate
>
> Strawberry
>
> Vanilla

Cool, now the buttons stack vertically, but they are a bit too close together.

Concatenating multiple break tags will increase the line separation between elements, because each **\
** starts a new line in the document:

```
<button type= "submit">Chocolate</button><br><br>
<button type= "submit">Strawberry</button><br><br>
<button type= "submit">Vanilla</button><br><br>
```

   Chocolate

   Strawberry

   Vanilla

Now the buttons have more elbow room, or, um, finger room.

If you're an online poet, you need **
** to format short lines that stack vertically on top of each other. Let's quote a bit of John Donne to illustrate the power of the line break:

No man is an island,
Entire of itself,
Every man is a piece of the continent,
A part of the main.
If a clod be washed away by the sea,
Europe is the less.
As well as if a promontory were.

<button>

Speaking of buttons! Now you know from the above example that an important way to make buttons in HTML is to declare "button" as the value to the **type** attribute of **<button>**. On the web there are many kinds of buttons, since this whole online interactivity thing seems to be based largely on the idea of clicking on lots of things. Thus, there is an infinity of ways to style buttons, you will be surprised (or maybe not). But since styling is for CSS, we will keep the button stylistics discussion to a minimum.

Buttons are built for style, though, so you can load them with additional content such as text and image, make them very colorful, round their corners, shadow their edges etc. They are crucial to the web because we need to click away to access online content. Given their importance on web pages, there will be some important attributes that specify or modify them in various ways to know about.

- **autofocus** Buttons can gain or lose 'focus' (losing focus is called 'blur'). Focus tells the browser to pay attention to the element because input might be coming from it. Its opposite, blur, might be used in a JavaScript function (note we are not discussing Js in this book) which tells the browser that data or an event has likely been run on the element and to verify this or simply lose focus now that the event has happened (clicking is an example of an event).

- **disabled** tells the browser to disable the button you have placed on your website. Hey, you might have your own reasons for giving users disabled buttons, I won't judge.

- **form** specifies the name of the form(s) it is associated with and takes as its declared value the name of the form. For example, you might use this within the **<button>** tag– **form= "coolForm"** – and then, in the HTML code, you have to give the attribute and value pairing **id= "coolForm"** within the **<form>** tag so that the button form attribute links to the **id** of the matching form element.

- **formaction** is used when you have set the type of the button to **submit** and takes as its value the URL where the form information has to be sent to once its Submit button has been clicked. This makes sense mainly at the end of a form to submit all the information in the form to whatever database server is waiting for it. Note that database servers are part of the back-end web infrastructure and so receiving form data is not covered in this book, as mentioned above in the Introduction.

- **formenctype** is only used when the button **type** attribute is set to **submit**. This tells the server receiving the information how the data should be encoded. The three possible values are: **application/x-www-form-urlencoded**, **multi-part/form-data**, and **text/plain**.

- **formmethod** is also for buttons with the **type** attribute set to **submit**. It takes one of two values, which indicate how to send the encoded data: **get and post**. This relates to servers and data, which is out of scope for this book.

- **formnovalidate** takes no additional value, and simply specifies that the form does not need to have its information validated by additional scripts being run on the data. This is only for buttons with the **type** attribute set to **submit**.

- **formtarget** For buttons with the **type** attribute set to **submit**, this attribute defines how form information should be displayed. The values are the same as for the **<a>** tag discussed above: **_blank, _self, _parent, _top, and framename**.

- **name** gives a name for the button.

- **type** is a more or less mandatory attribute, because browsers use different defaults as to the role a button is playing on the website. So kindly inform the browser, via the **type** attribute, whether it's value is of the **button, reset** or **submit** variety.

- **value** You can give an initial value to a button with this attribute. For example, you might have three buttons, for *chocolate, strawberry* and *vanilla*, and you are asking a user to select their favorite (of these three!) flavors. This allows you to put predefined data values into a button, so that that data gets sent when the button is clicked. These buttons might then look like this in the HTML:

```
<button type= "button" name="chooseFlavor"
value="choco">Chocolate<button><br><br>
<button type= "button" name="chooseFlavor"
value="straw">Strawberry<button><br><br>
<button type= "button" name="chooseFlavor"
value="vanil">Vanilla<button><br><br>
```

Above, we are sending the database abbreviations of our flavors, *choco, straw* and *vanil*. Databases don't need the full human-readable button labels that we place as content text between the opening and closing tags. For each button, the value is different. However, each button has the same name because they are all doing the same thing in a different respect– making us choose a flavor.

<canvas>

The Canvas is a rather amazing element, which is why it's capitalized at the start of this sentence. At first glance it looks like just another tag, but whole books have been written just on the HTML canvas element, because it specifies a rather feature rich place to create visual content in your HTML document. It is just like a canvas in painting– a place to paint your images! It defines a spatial container in your HTML document in which Canvas things happen. Some tags in HTML have 'superpowers' and Canvas is one of them. Another tag with superpower level abilities is **<script>** because running scripts on your website supercharges the possibilities for interactivity on your site. In fact, inside the **<canvas>** one runs specialized scripts to produce visual content that can even be interactive visual content.

In the example below, we create a Canvas, using its attributes of **width** and **height** to define in pixels its dimensions on the screen, and we give it a unique **id** (identifier attribute) which can be found by the JavaScript so that it knows where to draw our image. Our image is a simple blue-ish square. Technically it is not really "blue" but rather a particular kind of blue defined by its hex code value, which is **#3881f5.** A search engine result on "hex color html" will yield many an online resource for identifying narrowly defined color codes for your HTML, or you can use this link, http://bit.ly/MozHTMLcolor

With respect to the JavaScript below which draws the rectangle, you have already seen the coordinate system at work above in the **<area>** tag and its **coords** attribute. So the first pair of numbers gives the top left corner of the rectangle, and the second pair of numbers gives the bottom right coordinate. Since the script defines a 300 x 300-pixel square ,it easily fits inside the 500 x 500 canvas that has been set up for it. The drawing script accesses the **id** value **typicalCanvas** in order to draw in this particular canvas.

```
<!DOCTYPE html>
<html>
  <body>
    <canvas id="typicalCanvas" width="500px"
height="500px"></canvas>
```

```
<script>
  var canvas =
document.getElementById("typicalCanvas");
  var ctx = canvas.getContext("2d");
  ctx.fillStyle = "#3881f5";
  ctx.fillRect(10, 10, 360, 360);
</script>
</body>
</html>
```

*You define the canvas by giving it an **id** attribute that can be accessed by the drawing script, and **width** and **height** dimensions in which Canvas-drawn things occur.*

Because one actually draws in a Canvas using JavaScript, drawing is outside the scope of this book, but at least now you know about it and have one more cool reason to dive into JavaScript and explore the Canvas.

By the way, your Canvas can be quite large, ~33,000 pixels in both **width** x **height** in most browsers (~ 1 billion pixels, give or take a few), so paint away!

<caption>

<caption> is used to add a caption to tables, and by various publication traditions, tables have their captions placed just above the table, in contrast to figures, which have their captions placed beneath them. **<caption>** should always be the first child of a **<table>**, in honor of this tradition.

Below we have created a table for a simple Mediterranean style salad, yum and healthy. The bulk of the tags are **<table>**-related and so are discussed in more detail later (since we are progressing through the tags alphabetically). The main point to grasp here is that captions, if used, are placed in the HTML right after the **<table>** tag.

```
<!DOCTYPE html>
<html>
  <head>
    <style>
      table,
      th,
      td {
        border: 1px solid black;
      }
    </style>
  </head>
  <body>
    <table>
      <caption>Table caption area</caption>
      <tr>
        <th>Grocery Items</th>
        <th>Cost</th>
      </tr>
      <tr>
        <td>Cucumbers</td>
        <td>$6.50</td>
      </tr>
      <tr>
        <td>Tomatoes</td>
        <td>$7.00</td>
      </tr>
```

```
      <tr>
        <td>Olive Oil</td>
        <td>$13.50</td>
      </tr>
      <tr>
        <td>Feta</td>
        <td>$9.75</td>
      </tr>
    </table>
  </body>
</html>
```

Table caption area

Grocery Items	Cost
Cucumbers	$6.50
Tomatoes	$7.00
Olive Oil	$13.50
Feta	$9.75

Construction of a basic table showing where the `<caption>` *tag is placed.*

<cite>

Cite is used to indicate a moment in the HTML document where the title of some referenced creative work appears, such as referring to a film, book, court case, video game, painting, album and so on. Its usage is as follows:

```
<h2>Shark Films</h2>
    <p>
    One of the most famous shark movies of all time was
    <cite>Jaws</cite>.
    <p>
```

Text within a **<cite>** element will display as italicized by default.

<code>

Code elements define sections of computer code in an html document that are meant to be displayed to a user for them to read, as opposed to script being run in the browser to perform operations. Its syntax is as follows:

```
<code> var noodle = function() { // a function that
explains making noodles} </code>
```

<code> defaults to monospace text styling, which has kind of a computer code aesthetic.

<col> & <colgroup>

These tags belong together as part of the same general construct for creating columns. **<col>** has one attribute, **span**, which indicates how many columns the element should span across. Columns are self-closing and take no content directly, but rather affect the display of columns in a column group being used as part of a table (note that tables have their own tags, discussed below under **td, th** and **tr**).

```
<!DOCTYPE html>
<html>

  <body>
    <table>
```

```
      <colgroup>
        <col span="1" style="background-color:salmon">
        <col span="1" style="background-color:aqua">
        <col span="1" style="background-
color:LightGreen">
      </colgroup>
      <tr>
        <th>Salmon Stuff</th>
        <th>Aqua Stuff</th>
        <th>Green Stuff</th>
      </tr>
      <tr>
        <td>Smoked Sockeye</td>
        <td>Mediterranean</td>
        <td>Limes</td>
      </tr>
    </table>
  </body>
</html>
```

Salmon Stuff	Aqua Stuff	Green Stuff
Smoked Sockeye	Mediterranean	Limes

<col> being used to stylize the color of columns in a table

Above we have a table, which requires that in our current discussion we 'jump ahead' alphabetically to briefly summarize the table-related tags which are discussed later.

- **table** defines a table being set up.
- **th** is the tag for table headings.
- **tr** is the tag for rows of data.
- **td** can be thought of as 'table data' cells which are also called 'standard cells.'

We typically understand tables as comprised of rows and columns, since we are used to spreadsheets. Columns are not directly part of the table construct, however, because one can efficiently do without them as all one needs to do is define rows and cells. `<col>` and `<colgroup>` add additional column capacity to tables.

Since we want to color the columns in this example, it makes sense to express their HTML code first inside of `<table>`, so that the follow-on row sections of the table take on the specified color. Here we are using HTML color names instead of hex codes. Note that inside of a table, table heads will display as inline (horizontal) and table rows will display as block (vertical). In the column group section, we have given each column a span of 1, so that the colored categories span only 1 column. Higher numbers will span across more columns, but for illustration purposes, we are using three colors to indicate three different `<col>` color styles.

Three table headings are created, defining three kinds of 'stuff', with each connected to its **background-color** style: *Salmon, Aqua* and *Green*. With each heading, there is some data presented in the same order so that the data is visually connected to its heading: 'smoked sockeye' (goes with 'salmon'), 'Mediterranean' (goes with 'aqua') and 'Limes' (goes with 'Green').

The only attribute a column group has is **span**, which functions similarly to the same attribute in `<col>`. There are some ordering details to be aware of, since `<colgroup>` has to have `<table>` as its parent, be positioned after any `<caption>` tag, and before the other table elements.

<data>

The data tag is used to associate content with a data format, typically meant more for machine than human consumption. For example, if we were designing a website for a sock manufacturer, we might need to code something like:

```
<ol>
  <li><data value="48263553">White Socks</data></li>
  <li><data value="96342690">Red and White Striped
Socks</data></li>
  <li><data value="19839942">Black Socks</data></li>
  <li><data value="66623900">Grey Wool Socks</data></li>
  <li><data value="84519371">Recycled Socks</data></li>
  <li><data value="56775902">Velvet Socks</data></li>
</ol>
```

The value of a data tag can be accessed by JavaScript to perform various feats of database processing. If the machine-readable data you want to use relates to time, duration or date, use a **<time>** element instead.

<datalist>

Data lists work in tandem with the **<input>** and **<option>** tags to create a series of predefined options from which a selection can be made. The input is a text field which will show the items in the data list that best match the letters as they are being typed into the field. If no letters match, there will be no popup options to select from the data list. In the example below, if the user types "f" as the first character, "Alfa Romeo" will be shown in the popup, because it contains the letter "f."

```
<!DOCTYPE html>
<html>
  <body>
    <h2>Top Car Brands A-C</h2>
    <h3>Start typing letters beginning with A, B or
C</h3>

    <input list="topCarBrands">
    <datalist id="topCarBrands">
      <option value="Audi">
      <option value="Alfa Romeo">
      <option value="BMW">
      <option value="Bentley">
      <option value="Buick">
      <option value="Cadillac">
```

```
      <option value="Chevrolet">
      <option value="Chrysler">
    </datalist>
  </body>
</html>
```

Top Car Brands A-C

Start typing letters beginning with A, B or C

Typed in letters to the `<input>` field will show the car brands that contain the letter (if any)

<dd> , <dl> & <dt>

Like **<col>** and **<colgroup>, <dd>, <dl>** and **<dt>** work together to create description lists, which organize categories and items within them. **<dd>** can be thought of "description data" and may contain any kind of regular content within its opening and closing tags, such as text and images. This data is associated with a higher-level term which has a more general categorical importance, called a description term or **<dt>**.

```
<dl>
  <dt>Horror</dt>
    <dd>Stephen King</dd>
    <dd>John Carpenter</dd>
  <dt>Detective</dt>
    <dd>Sherlock Holmes</dd>
    <dd>True Detective</dd>
  <dt>Sci Fi</dt>
    <dd>Ursula Le Guin</dd>
    <dd>Arthur C. Clarke</dd>
</dl>
```

Horror
    Stephen King
    John Carpenter
Detective
    Sherlock Holmes
    True Detective
Sci Fi
    Ursula Le Guin
    Arthur C. Clarke

A description list.

<details> & <summary>

These tags work together to provide a nested list of elements that can be revealed by clicking on an arrow. **<summary>** provides a label for the hidden group of content, which can be any set of elements that relate conceptually to the summary field.

```
<details>
   <summary>Meet the Team!</summary>
   <p>Ermanno Immaculata, lead game designer</p>
   <p>Dionysios Aldo, business development</p>
   <p>Agata Pasqualina, intern</p>
   <p>Paraskevas Valente, sales</p>
</details>
```

▶ Meet the Team!

Inside <details> *we can see the* <summary> *at first.*

▼ Meet the Team!

Ermanno Immaculata, lead game designer

Dionysios Aldo, business development

Agata Pasqualina, intern

Paraskevas Valente, sales

If we click on the arrow, we see the hidden content!

Using the **open** attribute on **<details>** (open takes no additional value) will set the list to be open and visible by default, making it closable rather than openable. Together, **<details>** and **<summary>** construct what is known in web development as a "disclosure widget."

<dfn>

This tag marks up the defining instance of a term, which is a specialized word that makes its first appearance in a document. The style of text enclosed within **<dfn>** defaults to italicized.

```
<p>In audio, <dfn>white noise </dfn>refers to a random
signal comprised of all the audible frequencies played at
equal loudness.</p>
```

In audio, *white noise* refers to a random signal comprised of all the audible frequencies played at equal loudness.

Defining the first instance of a word.

<dialogue>

A dialogue tag usually contains content that is hidden, which is then revealed in its own box in the layout when activated by JavaScript. It can also take the attribute of open to display visibly by default. JavaScript is outside the scope of this book, and this element is typically used in tandem with Js.

<div>

A division tag creates a non-semantic section of content in the HTML document and displays in block (vertical) mode by default. It requires CSS to style it to make it visually apparent in the layout in some way beyond simply block display. In the example below, we have created two <div>s and styled them with some height and color information.

```
<style>
  div#one {
    height: 50px;
    background-color: red;
  }

  div#two {
    height: 50px;
    background-color: blue;
  }

</style>

<div id="one">

</div>

<div id="two">

</div>
```

Two <div>s, styled (color and size) based on their id.

<em>

Emphasis tags are used to create areas of text that should be emphasized in some way, for instance by targeting them for special stylization in CSS. **<em>** is part of a category of tags called *phrase tags* which include **<strong>, <code>, <samp>, <kbd>** and **<var>.** Phrase tags allow you to home in on particular categories of content so that you can give them a style treatment that emphasizes them differently from the main text on a site. Text enclosed within **<em>** tags will by default render as italicized. For example,

```
<p>Hey, I thought you said <em>this text should be
emphasized</em>, not merely italicized.</p>
```

will render as,

Hey, I thought you said *this text should be emphasized*, not merely italicized.

If you want to apply italics for the sake of italics, it is recommended that you use the **font-style** property in CSS with the value **italic**, to distinguish text that is merely italicized for visual reasons from text that is emphasized for content purposes. CSS is covered in the companion volume to this one. Similarly, **<i>** visually renders the same as **<em>** but lacks the semantic quality of 'being emphasized.'

<embed>

The embed tag allows you to embed other kinds of content within a defined area of the HTML page. It works as a plug-in section for connecting to other kinds of file and media types. For instance, if you want to embed Adobe Flash content into your web page, followed by an embedded video (because you are now inspired to embed lots of things!), you might write:

```
<embed src="flashFile.swf" type="application/x-shockwave-
flash" height="300px" width="500px">

<embed src="video.mp4" type="video/H264" height="300px"
width="500px">
```

This will create a 300 x 500-pixel area in which to embed your flash content, and a similar area for displaying a video file. The source (**src=**) of embedded media will be a URL of either a relative (file in a directory on your website server) or absolute kind (live on the web).

Aside from **<embed>'s** generally useful attributes such as **src, height** and **width**, it is important to use the **type** attribute to identify the media type being used. To see the full list of media types, visit `http://bit.ly/mediaTypes` as there are too many to list here. You will be truly amazed at how many media types there are!

Keep in mind that if you are wanting to use **<embed>** to create plug-in windows, a major trend in browser development these days is to remove plug-in support, since these can create major security risks.

<fieldset> & <legend>

When creating lists of controls or online forms, it is often useful to subdivide items into categorical groupings of related items. Fieldsets are sections of **<input>** items that define a grouping of data being requested from a user, while a **<legend>** defines the category of the input items.

```
<form>
  <fieldset>
    <legend>CONTACT INFORMATION</legend>
    Name: <input type="text"><br> <br>
    Email: <input type="text"><br> <br>
    Phone Number: <input type="text">
  </fieldset><br>
  <fieldset>
    <legend>EDUCATION</legend>
    Highest Degree: <input type="text"><br> <br>
    School: <input type="text"><br> <br>
    Graduation Date: <input type="text">
  </fieldset><br>
  <fieldset>
    <legend>WORK HISTORY</legend>
    Current Employer: <input type="text"><br> <br>
    Responsibilities: <input type="text"><br> <br>
    Dates of Employment: <input type="text">
  </fieldset>
</form>
```

Sections of a form defined by a `<legend>` for each section, with default black border styling for each `<fieldset>`.

`<figcaption>` & `<figure>`

Images are often published with a caption beneath them providing additional context. A figure differs functionally from other kinds of images on a website, since they are usually referenced in the surrounding text. For example, in a paragraph an author might write, "...see Figure 1" and in the overall context of the content, figures proceed sequentially as illustrations of what is being discussed in the text. A figure caption might be as simple as, "Fig. 1. An archaeological dig site in Crete."

```
<figure class="cityImages">
    <img src="http://bit.ly/33y4EuS" width="300"
    height="300" alt="city" draggable=false>
</figure>
<figcaption style="text-align:left">Fig. 1. One of many
cities in the database of City Images.</figcaption>
```

Fig. 1. One of many cities in the database of City Images.

<figcaption> and *<figure>* used together.

A complete **<figure>** element consists of the parent figure tags, with **<img>** and optional **<figcaption>** elements inside.

<footer>

A footer is information shown at the bottom of its content container. An entire website might have a footer, or just one isolated section of it. Below, we have redefined the information of the city photo from a figure caption to a footer, which contains typical footer information such as creative and copyright indications.

```
<figure class="cityImages">
    <img src="http://bit.ly/33y4EuS" width="300"
height="300">
    </figure>
    <footer>
      <p>Photo Credit: Chloe Camera Whiz</p>
      <p>Chloe's photo portfolio <a
href="chloephoto.com">Chloe
      Photo</a>.</p>
      <p>Copyright 2020</p>
    </footer>
```

Photo Credit: Chloe Camera Whiz

Chloe's photo portfolio Chloe Photo.

A footer at the bottom of a photo gallery.

\<form\>

Forms are for collecting information directly from site visitors who are providing their information voluntarily. There are many other tags that can go into a form. We've seen some of them, but here is a more complete list: `<input>`, `<textarea>`, `<button>`, `<select>`, `<option>`, `<optgroup>`, `<fieldset>`, `<label>`, and `<output>`. Given how ubiquitous forms are on the internet, it isn't surprising that this tag has a significant list of attributes for customizing its usage on a web page. The attributes a form can take are summarized below.

- **accept-charset** The character set refers to the information coming into the document from the keyboard. The default for this attribute is UNKNOWN, which means it will take its marching orders from the surrounding context. The most commonly used character sets are UTF-8 and ISO-8859-1, which are the character sets for Unicode and the Latin alphabet, respectively.

- **action** tells the form what to do with the information after it has been submitted, by taking a URL where the data is sent to.

- **autocomplete** can be take the values **on** or **off**. This tells the browser whether or not to automatically fill in similar information that has been typed before.

- **enctype** is used when the **method** attribute has its value set to **post**. It defines the data encoding type and can have its value sent to **application/x-www-form-urlencoded**, **multipart/form-data** or **text/plain**. Which method you choose depends on your backend architecture for handling form data, which is outside this book's scope.

- **method** has two values, which indicate which HTTP method to use for sending data, **get** or **post**. Which method you choose depends on your backend architecture for handling form data.

- **name** is used to give the form a specific name or to give unique names to elements within the form.

- **novalidate** does not need an additional value and simply declares that the information in the form does not need to be validated.

- **target** takes the same values we've seen before with other tags that allow for specification of opening pages, **_blank, _self, _parent,** and **_top.** It is used to present the follow-on page once a form has been submitted.

```
<form method="get" enctype="application/x-www-form-
urlencoded" action="/html/codes/html_form_handler.cfm">
  <fieldset>
    <legend>Which show do you want to see?</legend>
    <p><label> <input type="radio" name="firstShow"> 7pm
</label></p>
    <p><label> <input type="radio" name="secondShow"> 9pm
</label></p>
    <p><label> <input type="radio" name="thirdShow"> 11pm
</label></p>
  </fieldset>
  <br>
  <fieldset>
    <legend>Additional Purchases</legend>
```

```
    <p><label> <input type="checkbox" name="addons"
value="snackPop">Popcorn</label></p>
    <p><label> <input type="checkbox" name="addons"
value="swagWear">T-Shirt</label></p>
    <p><label> <input type="checkbox" name="addons"
value="sweet">Candy</label></p>
  </fieldset>
  <p><button>Submit Now</button></p>
</form>
```

─Which show do you want to see?─

○ 7pm

○ 9pm

○ 11pm

─Additional Purchases─────────

☐ Popcorn

☐ T-Shirt

☐ Candy

Submit Now

A <form> example.

<h1> - <h6> & <hgroup>

These tags refer to different levels of headings that might be used to organize textual content. Typically headings declare in a relatively small number of words some major section topic that delineates a page's content. **<hgroup>** has been removed from HTML5 but is still used and frequently appears in other online HTML5 references, and so is included here just to illustrate how it might be used.

```
<hgroup>
  <h1>Heading 1</h1>
  <p>Paragraph under a heading.</p>
  <h2>Heading 2</h2>
  <p>Paragraph under a heading.</p>
  <h3>Heading 3</h3>
  <p>Paragraph under a heading.</p>
  <h4>Heading 4</h4>
  <p>Paragraph under a heading.</p>
  <h5>Heading 5</h5>
  <p>Paragraph under a heading.</p>
  <h6>Heading 6</h6>
  <p>Paragraph under a heading.</p>
</hgroup>
```

Heading 1

Paragraph under a heading.

Heading 2

Paragraph under a heading.

Heading 3

Paragraph under a heading.

Heading 4

Paragraph under a heading.

Heading 5

Paragraph under a heading.

Heading 6

Paragraph under a heading.

A demonstration of all six heading levels relative to a standard paragraph element.

`<hgroup>` by itself doesn't produce any visual change.

\<head\>

The head section of an html document is placed above the body of the document, just under the **\<html\>** tag. There is no requirement to have a head section, but it usually makes a lot of sense to have one. It is especially important for containing machine-readable information that browsers need in order to deliver web sites effectively. The head is where you want to **\<link\>** to stylesheets, place **\<meta\>** tags, add some useful **\<script\>**s, give the page a **\<title\>**, and in general provide code that affects or describes the page as a whole but doesn't actually comprise its main content, since that would go in the **\<body\>** section of the document, instead.

```
<!DOCTYPE html>
<html>
<head>
  <title>Page Title</title>
  <meta>
  <script></script>
</head>
<body>
  Main document content
</body>
```

\<header\>

A header is the opposite of a footer– it encapsulates content that is placed at the top of a section, rather than at the bottom of it, typically serving introductory purposes. It can include images, headings, paragraphs, navigation, logo, author identification, and other kinds of content that would make sense in a header section.

\<hr\>

This is the horizontal rule tag. It is used to create clean section breaks in a document by drawing a line to separate them. Horizontal rules are often employed when there is some kind of major topic or thematic change in the content. With CSS you can style **\<hr\>** far beyond a simple black dividing line.

```
<p>Here is one thematic section</p>
<hr>
<p>Let's make a clean break with that section, and start
a whole new theme</p>
```

Here is one thematic section

Let's make a clean break with that section, and start a whole new theme

Use of the \<hr\> tag.

\<html\>

With the exception of the !DOCTYPE declaration, all the text in an HTML document must be expressed inside of the opening and closing **\<html\>** tags. The HTML tag is the parent tag that defines the entire document of any HTML page. **\<html\>** is thus considered to be the *root element* since it is located at the top level of the parent/child hierarchy that makes up a web document's tree structure.

<i>

This is the italics tag which it does not have a semantic quality to it, other than declaring that it is being used to visually present text in a way that's different from the surrounding context. Other tags also display italicized text but do so with explicit semantic purpose, such as `<em>` and `<cite>`. `<i>` simply makes text italicized but gives no semantic reason in its placement and usage for doing so.

```
<p>This text is <i>not</i> italicized except for the
<i>not</i>.
```

This text is *not* italicized except for the *not*.

<iframe>

An `<iframe>` is an inline frame. It is typically used to show some content from another website, such as when one embeds a YouTube or Google Map link into a website (it is kind of like a little 'window' onto the other site). To illustrate, here is some HTML featuring non-existent website URLs, which will produce web frowny faces because these sites do not actually exist.

```
<iframe src="https://www.blanknothing.info"></iframe>
<iframe src="https://www.theyrehere.net"></iframe>
<iframe src="https://www.zaworld.info"></iframe>
```

Frowny `<iframe>` *results because we are trying to render non-existent websites.*

Besides **src**, other attributes include **height** and **width** (which we are now very familiar with), **name** (in case we want to name an iframe), and two new attributes that we haven't seen yet, **srcdoc** and **sandbox**.

srcdoc allows us to provide content for an iframe that is actually internal to the html document, rather than linking to an external URL. Here's an example of **srcdoc** adding content to an iframe from the HTML document itself.

```
<iframe srcdoc="<p>Let's put some text onto our website
inside of an iframe!</p>"></iframe>

<iframe srcdoc="<h1>Let's put a heading inside of an
iframe!</h1>"></iframe>
```

Let's put some text onto our website inside of an iframe!	# Let's put a heading inside of an iframe!

Adding content to an `<iframe>` from within the page's HTML.

The **sandbox** attribute in an iframe puts a set of restrictions onto the content inside of it, such as disabling APIs and scripts, preventing the use of plugins or targeting by other elements on the website, blocking automatic triggering and in general clamps down on what's possible to do with the content in an iframe. Using the attribute just by itself enforces the full set of restrictions. It is also possible to lift certain restrictions by allowing each one individually. The syntax for this would be:

```
<iframe sandbox= "allow-popups allow-scripts">
```

Each permission is explicitly defined and separated by a space. The full list of permissions can be found at `http://bit.ly/SandboxAllow`

Outside of the **sandbox**, allowances can also be declared using **allow** as an attributed which takes as its value a feature policy. Feature values that can be allowed include **accelerometer, camera, geolocation, microphone, midi** and **speaker** amongst others, e.g. allow="camera". For a complete list of features that can be allowed, see http://bit.ly/allowFeatures

Finally, a common use of **<iframe>** is to embed maps onto a page. You can copy the embed code from Google Maps, for example, and paste the **<iframe>** element into your HTML:

```
<iframe
src="https://www.google.com/maps/embed?pb=!1m18!1m12!1m3!
1d46731.83463789939!2d-
122.14235937522655!3d42.94161489584187!2m3!1f0!2f0!3f0!3m
2!1i1024!2i768!4f13.1!3m3!1m2!1s0x54c63e84c023ab41%3A0xba
e1bf19c88b877a!2sCrater%20Lake!5e0!3m2!1sen!2sca!4v157375
0571513!5m2!1sen!2sca" width="600" height="450"
frameborder="0" style="border:0;"
allowfullscreen=""></iframe>
```

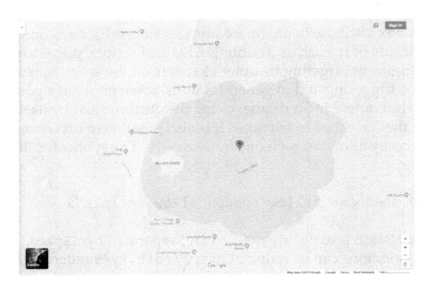

A Google Maps **<iframe>** *embed.*

To get the embed code from Google Maps, go to Google Maps and type in a destination. Then, click on the hamburger menu, which looks like this:

—

A hamburger menu icon in a browser.

In the menu select *Share or embed map*, which has a link icon. This will give you two options, *Send a link* and *Embed a map*. You want to second option, which will give you the `<iframe>` code to paste into your HTML document. You can make adjustments to this code as you need to, for instance by changing the width and height dimensions.

<img>

We have already seen the image tag in action. It is a self-closing tag in which all the pertinent information for presenting the image in a structural way (as opposed to a stylized way, which is the job of CSS) in included as `attribute="value"` pairs. In this example, we have packed an **<img>** with lots of attributes!

```
<img  alt="city" corssorigin="anonymous" ismap
longdesc="http://longdescription.com"
src="http://bit.ly/33y4EuS" sizes="min-w usemap="#city"
width="300" height="300">
```

Some of these we've seen before, but some are new. We shouldn't by now need to explain **alt**, **src**, **usemap** (this was covered in **<area>** above), **width** and **height.** Note, however, that since **<img>** is self-closing, it does require the **src** attribute in order to identify the actual image to be shown. So let's briefly discuss the other attributes.

ismap is the server-side version of **usemap**. **ismap** and **usemap** break down along the frontend/backend (or client side/server side) distinction we discussed in the Introduction. **usemap** creates the ability to map regions from within a user's browser (who is always a front-end client). **ismap** allows an application running in the back end, on a server, to map an image into regions.

longdesc provides a URL link (either a relative or absolute) to a longer description of the image.

The **crossorigin** attribute has to do with controlling the manner in which we allow other websites, which are at different origins, access to fetch data from the current one. There are security implications to servers fetching data from the site, which is a back-end topic out of scope here. The two values it accepts are **anonymous** and **use-credentials**.

Here are the main supported image types, listed by their name, Media Type, and file extension.

```
APNG        image/apng        .apng
BMP         image/bmp         .bmp
GIF         image/gif         .gif
ICO         image/x-icon      .ico or .cur
JPEG        image/jpeg        .jpg, .jpeg
PNG         image/png         .png
SVG         image/svg+xml     .svg
TIFF        image/tiff        .tif, .tiff
```

Because loading an image onto a screen generally takes longer than loading text, you have some control over how image loading affects overall page loading. The decoding attribute lets you define this behavior more specifically and takes these values:

- **sync** the image will load when the browser comes to the image information in the source code.

- **async** the browser will process the image loading out of sync with loading the rest of the content.

- **auto** lets the browser decide the best way to load images relative to the rest of the content.

<input>

Input tags are used inside of forms to collect data from users. Given the high importance of collecting information from users on websites, we should not be surprised to see many attributes giving fine tuning control over this tag. Input tags are self-closing and only have attributes. Note that to fully use forms, some backend technologies are needed, such as PHP or JavaScript which will actually place from data into a database. HTML only provides content containers for this information and does not execute code directly onto a database.

accept is used in conjunction with the **file** attribute to define what kinds of files may be uploaded. **file** defines the kind of file that is wanted but **accept** filters out all the other file types except for the ones that it takes as its value. In the example below, we place a restriction on the file type that we want uploaded to those with a **.png** file extension.

```
<form>
  <input type="file" accept=".png">
</form>
```

Choose File   No file chosen

A file upload input.

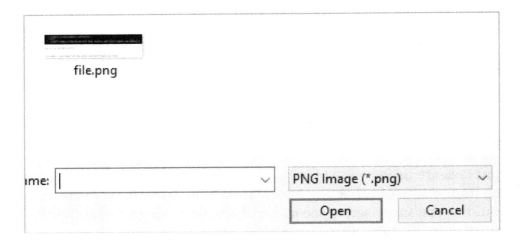

file.png

ime: | PNG Image (*.png)

Open   Cancel

PNG files only, please.

- **alt** we've seen before– it just gives an alternate name for displayed visual content, in this case a form.

- **autocomplete** we've also seen before. It tells the browser whether or not to fill in the form based on similar information filled in previously.

- **autofocus** takes no explicit value and tells the browser to automatically give the input focus.

- **checked** displays an already checked checkbox as the input.

- **dirname** allows the text direction info to be submitted with the data. The input has to be given a name first, and then the value format for dirname is **inputname.dir**

- **disabled** allows you to disable an input, which might be useful if you want certain conditions to be met before making it usable.

- **form** lets you give and send the name of the form that the input belongs to as part of the data it can send. For this to work, the form needs to have a value in its **name** attribute. This name is then used by the input's form attribute using the value **name_id**

- **formaction** gives the URL that the input will be sent to.

- **formenctype** we've seen before. It gives the data encoding type, and takes the possible values **application/x-www-form-urlencoded, multipart/form-data** and **text/plain**

- **formnovalidate** indicates that input validation is not needed (e.g. to see if the data is formatted in a certain way). For instance, JavaScript or PHP might want to make sure that a US zip code has five numbers entered.

- **formtarget** takes familiar values we've seen, **_blank, _self, _parent, _top.**

- **formmethod** is either **get** or **post**, as seen earlier.

- **height, width, src, value, name** we have already become familiar with.

- **list** is used if there is a predefined datalist as part of the form. It takes the attribute structure **datalist_id**

- **max** and **min** give either a maximum or minimum value for a data input and is either a date or a number.

- **maxlength** takes a number as its value and specifies a maximum number of characters that can be used in the input field.

- **multiple** takes no additional value and allows a user to make more than one data entry in a field.

- **pattern** takes regular expressions as its input. A full discussion of regular expressions is out of scope for this book.

- **placeholder** is a hint that is pre-placed in the field, letting the user know the kind of information being asked for. Its value is the text to occupy the field temporarily before the user starts typing in it.

- **required** takes no additional value and makes the input field required for sending the form.

- **size** gives the width of an **<input>** element, specified in number of characters.

- **step** allows one to control the step increments of input numbers to make them acceptable to a form. It takes a number as a value, e.g. if set to 4, then all numbers must be multiples of 4: 0, 4, 8, 12, 16 etc.

- **type** specifies the type of input it is. The possible types are **button, checkbox, color, date, datetime-local,** email, file, hidden, image, month, number, password, radio, range, reset, search, submit, tel, text, time, url and week. Two of these types, radio and checkbox, are shown below.

```
<form>
  <p>
    Vacation Locations</p>
  <input type="checkbox" name="vacation">Italy<br>
  <input type="checkbox" name="vacation">Thailand<br>
  <input type="checkbox" name="vacation">Kenya<br>
  <input type="checkbox" name="vacation">Florida<br>
  <p>Ways to get there.</p>
  <input name="vehicular" type="radio">Plane<br>
  <input name="vehicular" type="radio">Train<br>
  <input name="vehicular" type="radio">Cruise<br>
  <input name="vehicular" type="radio">Blimp<br><br>
  <input type="submit" value="Submit">
</form>
```

Vacation Locations

- Italy
- Thailand
- Kenya
- Florida

Ways to get there.

- Plane
- Train
- Cruise
- Blimp

Submit

Checkboxes and radio buttons as the type of an input.

<ins> & <del>

The **<del>** tag allows you to show text that has been deleted (which is rendered as a strikethrough), while **<ins>** is the insert tag that shows the new text that has been added (rendered as underlined). These can function analogously to Track Changes tools in word processor documents. Note that these stylings of strikethrough and underline, for **<del>** and **<ins>** respectively, are defaults that can be changed with CSS.

```
<p>I prefer reading <del>paperbacks</del>
<ins>ebooks</ins>!</p>.
```

I prefer reading ~~paperbacks~~ <u>ebooks</u>!

<kbd>

This tag stands for 'keyboard' and indicates that text has been received from a keyboard or other text entry device including voice recognition systems. Like **<code>** it defaults to monospace text styling.

```
<p>This message came in through the online chat:
<kbd>Hello, I need to schedule a repair.</kbd></p>
```

<label>

Labels provide names for **<form>** input types. Below, we have a typical in-flight meal selection presented as raw HTML.

```
<form>
   <h2>Your Meal Preference for this Flight</h2>
   <label for="male">Chicken and Mushroom Sauce</label>
   <input type="radio" name="choice" class="flightMeal"
value="chicken"><br>
```

```
  <label for="female">Beef and Broccoli</label>
  <input type="radio" name="choice" class="flightMeal"
value="beef"><br>
  <label for="other">Veggie Pasta</label>
  <input type="radio" name="choice" class="flightMeal"
value="veggie"><br><br>
  <input type="submit" value="We're On It!">
</form>
```

Your Meal Preference for this Flight

Chicken and Mushroom Sauce
Beef and Broccoli
Veggie Pasta

We're On It!

Labels with radio buttons.

Labels can be given for each element in a form, or for an entire form. To specify what kind of label is being used, **<label>** takes two attributes, with the syntax **for="element_id"** or **form="form_id"** respectively. Labels increase the clickable size area of the input elements they are associated with, since they can be clicked on as well, being connected to the interactive aspect of the input type.

<li>, <ul> & <ol>

The list-related tags produce either ordered or unordered lists, **<ol>** or **<ul>** respectively, in your HTML page, both of which take list items **<li>**. Unordered lists have bulleted list items, whereas ordered lists have list items that are numbered. Ordered lists default to an ascending numerical order but this can be changed, as shown below.

```
<h3>Today's To-Do List</h3>
<ol>
  <li>Make Coffee</li>
  <li>Uber our child to school.</li>
  <li>Massage</li>
</ol>
<br>
<h3>Canadian Political Parties</h3>
<ul>
  <li>Conservative</li>
  <li>Green</li>
  <li>Liberal</li>
  <li>NDP</li>
</ul>
```

Today's To-Do List

1. Make Coffee
2. Uber our child to school.
3. Massage

Canadian Political Parties

- Conservative
- Green
- Liberal
- NDP

Ordered and Unordered Lists

Unordered lists have no attributes, but you can, for instance, take control of the bullet points with CSS (a topic covered in the follow-on book to this one).

List items (**<li>**) do have one attribute, **value**, which allows you to start the numbering at a particular value, and then the subsequent items in the list will increment up from there. For example:

```
<h3>Favorite Movies #100 to #200</h3>
<ol>
 <li value="100">Alien</li>
 <li>Jaws</li>
 <li>Driving Miss Daisy</li>
</ol>
<br>
```

Favorite Movies #100 to #200

100. Alien
101. Jaws
102. Driving Miss Daisy

Starting an <ol> at a number given in the value attribute.

Ordered lists have the most attributes of this tag set, allowing you to specify the **type** of list item identifier, decide which number to **start** at, and giving you the ability to have the list items presented in **reversed** order. To push these attributes in an odd direction to really clarify the concept of how these attributes work, let's look at this strange example of a list you would probably never create (but should know about in case a client ever asks for such an odd list-beast!).

```
<h3>Let's Start at V and Work Our Way Backwards</h3>
<ol type="a" start="22" reversed>
  <li value="v">Victory at Last</li>
  <li>Uber my child to school please</li>
  <li>Tomtom</li>
  <li>Somewhere is a Rainbow</li>
  <li>Rise of the Fallen</li>
  <li>Quantum Qbits</li>
  <li>Powder Keg</li>
</ol>
<br>
```

Let's Start at V and Work Our Way Backwards

v. Victory at Last
u. Uber my child to school please
t. Tomtom
s. Somewhere is a Rainbow
r. Rise of the Fallen
q. Quantum Qbits
p. Powder Keg

Starting at a letter and counting backwards from it, letter-wise

So what's going on here in this backwards letter counting ordered list? First, we have some attributes declared in the **<ol>** tag and then a follow-on attribute in the subsequent **<li>** tag that makes this work. The first attribute is **type= "a"**. The values for type in **<ol>** specify how you would like to go about counting and ordering the list items. Your choices are:

1 for numbers
A for capital letters
a for lowercase letters
I or **i** for Roman numerals in uppercase or lowercase (good luck when you get over #50 or 'L' or 'l'. BTW did you know that the Romans invented uppercase and lowercase in the first place?)

So **type="a"** tells the browser that we want an ordering system based on lowercase letters. **start** specifies where to begin the count, and it always takes a Roman number so if you want letters, you'll have to figure out its number place in the Latin alphabet. The **<h3>** heading text says we want to start at 'V' so that letter is #22 in the alphabet.

Just for fun we have decided to make the whole list go backwards by using the **reversed** attribute which takes no additional value. Finally, **value** in the first **<li>** sets the starting place for the first list item, from which the remaining items take their marching orders.

<link>

Link tags (their full name is "HTML External Resource Link Elements"!) are for linking the HTML document to external resources, such as other files that contain CSS styling or that present visual icons. These are self-closing tags which take only attributes. For example, if we wanted to link to an external stylesheet, we would write the following code in the **<head>** at the top of the document:

```
<link rel="stylesheet" type="text/css"
href="CSSstyle.css">
```

As you may remember from the Introduction, all source code files are just text files at heart, so **type** indicates what kind of code is on this linked text file. We've seen many of the attributes **<link>** uses before, so we will not delve into these ones again: **crossorigin, href, hreflang, sizes** and **type**. It's worth revisiting the media attribute in the **<a>** section for values that pertain similarly to **<link>**. We will focus here on **rel**, which has some important **<link>** specificity.

rel is a required attribute for **<link>** and indicates the relationship of the linked resource to the HTML document. Here are the various kinds of relationships that can be declared between an HTML document and its linked resource.

- **alternate** is for alternate versions of the same document, which could be in different formats, that are linked to via a URL.

- **author** takes a URL for author's information.

- **canonical** An attribute that indicates the link is to the official or most preferred version of the content.

- **dns-prefetch** is used for DNS (domain name system) purposes by a server.

- **help** takes a URL for a help resource.

- **icon** is used for visual image resources.

- **license** gives a link to copyright and licensing kinds of info.

- **next** takes the URL of the next document in a sequence.

- **pingback** gives the IP address for a pingback server.

- **preconnect** tells the browser to connect to the linked resource's origin.

- **prefetch** tells the browser to cache the resource as it is likely to be needed.

- **preload** instructs the browser to prefetch and load the resource into cache.

- **prerender** tells the browser to dedicate some of its processing resources to preload another linked web page so that it will launch faster if the user navigates to it.

- **prev** is the opposite of **next** above and refers to the previous document in a series.

- **search** links to a resource that can provide a search function on the document for a user.

- **stylesheet** takes the URL for a CSS stylesheet that is being used to stylize the document.

It should be clear that many if not most of these rel values are for backend server-side operations that are out of scope for this book.

\<main\>

Main is a tag that can 'embrace' a lot of other tags that make up the most important section of a website. For instance, it can contain a gallery, a series of articles or blog posts, tables and so on that would be considered as the most important content on a page. It's essentially a wrapper tag that becomes a parent element to any of the other HTML tags enclosed within it. Because it represents the main content on a page, there shouldn't be more than one **\<main\>** on a page.

\<map\>

Map we have seen in action above in the **\<area\>** section. It defines on the client (frontend, user) side a way to make areas within images clickable and works in tandem with the **usemap** attribute of **\<img\>**. Each **\<area\>** element, which is enclosed within **\<map\>**, defines the coordinates of a clickable area in the image map. **\<map\>** has a required **name** attribute, since it must be given a name to be usable.

\<mark\>

The mark tag allows you to highlight passages of content. It defaults to yellow, but you can of course use CSS to provide a much wider array of highlighter colors, similar to what you might find at office supply stores.

```
<p>It is very important that when you study a lot, you
<mark>highlight</mark> all the important parts of the
book to score better on the test.</p>
```

It is very important that when you study a lot, you highlight all the
important parts of the book to score better on the test.

Highlighting text with <mark>.

<meta>

Meta tags embed metadata about your web page inside the **<head>**
section that does not display on the page itself but can be read by
search engines and various web applications. Typical uses of meta tags
are to help with SEO (search engine optimization) by providing
additional keywords, descriptions, author and modification
information about the site. There is also an attribute for defining the
page width to be in relation to the size of the display screen that is
viewing it. For example, to set a page to show its content up the edges
of the device it is being viewed on, one would include this code in the
<head>, which says that the HTML content has its **width=** to the width
of the viewing device's screen:

```
<meta name="viewport" content="initial-scale=1.0,
width=device-width">
```

The **name** attribute of **<meta>** does a lot of work, since it defines the
kind of content that is placed within the **content** attribute of the same
<meta> tag. For example:

```
  <meta name="author" content="Demon Dog Joe">
  <meta name="description" content="Best Hot Dogs in
Chicago!">
  <meta name="keywords" content="hoagey, ketchup,
mustard, relish, footlong">
```

Descriptions are the short lines of text that appear under the main result on a web search that turns up your site. They are very important to SEO because they are scanned by users as they are considering whether or not to click on your link. Keywords were highly abused in the early days of the web, as many millions of people thought that they could just load up on clever keywords to try to trick browsers into boosting their rank on a search result page. Today's search algorithms are cleverer than today's keyword abusers, so just use these honestly to give extra machine-readable insight into your page's content or purpose.

Other **\<meta\>** attributes, such as **charset** and **http-equiv**, have primarily server-side implications (we have also discussed **charset** earlier). Other name values that we haven't yet mentioned are **generator** (which describes which software, if any, may have been used to create the web page) and **application-name** (which is used if the web page is also a web application, and thus might need a name, e.g. if you have a travel booking site, you would put its name here as the value).

<meter>

The meter tag gives you a handy tool for presenting data in a level meter format, also known as a scalar data representation.

```
<h2>Are We There Yet??</h2>
<meter value="50" min="0" max="100"></meter><br>
<p>halfway there!</p>
<h2>Are We There Yet???</h2>
<meter value="0.75"></meter>
<p>50% more of halfway there!</p>
```

Are We There Yet??

halfway there!

Are We There Yet???

50% more of halfway there!

<meter> can obviously become much more visually compelling when animated by real-time JavaScript and stylized in CSS.

Within the minimum and maximum range, we can also define ranges based on the attributes of **low, optimal** and **high**, which take numbers as the values defining them. Based on the value data, there will be default color coding applied to the level meter of red, yellow and green to give a visual indication of which range we are in.

```
<label for="cash">Cash in Checking Account:</label>
<meter id="money"
       min="0" max="1000"
       low="100" high="900" optimum="1000"
       value="199">
</meter>
```

Cash in Checking Account:

*Color coded ranges using **hi, low** and **optimal** attributes in addition to **min** and **max**.*

<nav>

You might think that given how important navigation is on websites (moving around to different parts of the information contained on them), that **<nav>** might be one of the more complicated tags, but it is far from being so. Navigation items are usually just links, as in the **<a>** tag, or a set of **<li>**s inside of **<ol>**s or **<ul>**s. One of the reasons to decide which kind of these navigation content items, links or lists, to use is whether you want the links showing as inline or block display.

```
<nav>
  <a href="#home">Home</a>
  <a href="#about">About</a>
  <a href="#food">Menu</a>
  <a href="#where">Location</a>
  <a href="#jobs">We're Hiring!</a>
</nav>
<br>
<nav>
  <ul>
    <li><a href="#home">Home</a></li>
    <li><a href="#about">About</a></li>
    <li><a href="#food">Menu</a></li>
    <li><a href="#where">Location</a></li>
    <li><a href="#jobs">We're Hiring!</a></li>
  </ul>
</nav>
```

Home About Menu Location We're Hiring!

- Home
- About
- Menu
- Location
- We're Hiring!

Inline and block display nav items.

It is not necessary to have navigation links enclosed within **<nav>** tags, since any link can be used to navigate to content. **<nav>** is used mainly to create a major block of navigation components, and pages can have more than one **<nav>** area.

To create a multi-page website, the URL in your navigation links will express a relative path to the file name of the other pages you want the user to navigate to. Below is an example of what the files and directories inside of a pub_html server directory might look like for a multi-page website, and how to link to these other pages with the **href** attribute in **<a>.**

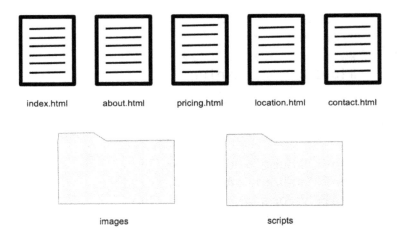

Files and assets comprising a multi-page website.

The links in the **<nav>** element would simply express a relative path to these other .html files in the **href** attribute in the anchor element.

```
<li><a href="index.html">Home</a></li>
<li><a href="about.html">About</a></li>
<li><a href="pricing.html">Menu</a></li>
<li><a href="location.html">Location</a></li>
<li><a href="contact.html">We're Hiring!</a></li>
```

<noscript>

Content inside of this tag is presented to a user if their browser has client-side scripts disabled or if for some reason they are using a browser that cannot handle the JavaScript being used. For example:

```
<script> <!-- some very cool script we wrote -->
</script>
<noscript> Darn, we went through all this trouble to
write some great JavaScript, but you have disabled
scripts in your browser : (    </noscript>
```

<object> & <param>

The object tag is similar to **<embed>** and **<iframe>** as it provides another way to embed content from another website or application into your page. In fact, there is a lot of confusion in the online forums as to why there are both **<embed>** and **<object>** tags. Some developers claim that embed is old and object is new, while others claim that embed was "resurrected" for HTML5! Here is an example of how to use **<object>** to embed an audio file (taken from http://bit.ly/objCite).

```
<object type="audio/x-wav" data="data/test.wav"
width="250" height="40">
   <param name="src" value="data/sound.wav">
   <param name="autoplay" value="false">
   <param name="autoStart" value="0">
   alt : <a href="data/test.wav">sound.wav</a>
</object>
```

<object> takes attributes we have seen before and so will just mention them here: **data, form, height, name, type, usempa,** and **width.**

It also has a **data** attribute that takes a URL (either absolute or relative) which holds the data to be displayed in its very **<embed>**- and **<iframe>**- like frame.

Some kinds of content embedded with **\<object>** have parameters, which can be defined and controlled with the **\<param>** tag. For example, if there is audio embedded in an **\<object>**, then

```
<param name="autoplay" value="true">
```

This will play the sound on page load without needing to be explicitly started by the user. As shown here, **\<param>** has attributes of **name** and **value** to specify the values that should be applied to the parameters of the content embedded in the **\<object>**.

Another use case might be to display a scrollable PDF resource on your page. Let's say that we found a great Open Access *PLOS One* article on cows that you have downloaded and placed in an 'assets' folder and given a simple name to (cow article source: `http://bit.ly/PLOScow`), your HTML might look something like this:

```
<object type="application/pdf" data="assets/PDF.pdf"
height="600" width="300"></object>
```

Using `<object>` to present a scrollable PDF resource on a web page.

<optgroup> & <option>

These tags can work together with **`<select>`** to present a user with a well-organized set of options to choose from, in a popup window format. A set of **`<option>`** tags will present a user with a list of options, while this option set can also be organized into categories of options by nesting them within **`<optgroup>`** tags.

```
<h2>
  Genetically Engineer Your Baby with CRISPR</h2>
<h3>Enhancements Alphabetically</h3>
<select>
  <option>Bioluminescence</option>
```

```
  <option>Blue Eyes</option>
  <option>No Freckles</option>
  <option>Super Strength</option>
  <option>X-Ray Vision</option>
</select>
<br><br>
<h3>Enhancements by Category</h3>
<select>
  <optgroup label="Eyes">
    <option>Blue Eyes</option>
    <option>X-Ray Vision</option>
  </optgroup>
  <optgroup label="Physical">
    <option>Super Speed</option>
    <option>Super Strength</option>
  </optgroup>
</select>
```

Genetically Engineer Your Baby with CRISPR

Enhancements Alphabetically

Enhancements by Category

Blue Eyes

Both present popup windows and seem very similar at first.

When the dropdown menu is selected, they present the options differently, either without or within additional categorical distinctions.

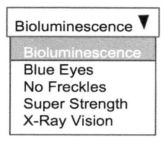 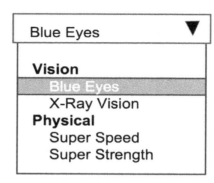

Presenting options without or with option groupings.

<optgroup> has a **disabled** attribute (no additional value) to disable the set of options, and a **label** attribute for giving the group a name. **<option>** has these same attributes but also **value** to send data to a server and **select** presents options that have been preselected (sort of like when you book flights or theater tickets and some seats have already been preselected for you).

<output>

The output tag can display the results of calculations or other interactions. Below, some JavaScript is being used on a **<form>** element to produce a mathematical addition operation between two different input elements, one being a slider and the other a text field where a value can be entered. The result of the calculation is displayed in the **<output>** element. The code below came from http://bit.ly/MozOutput

```
<form
oninput="result.value=parseInt(a.value)+parseInt(b.value)
">
  <input type="range" name="b" value="50" /> +
  <input type="number" name="a" value="10" /> =
  <output name="result">60</output>
</form>
```

+ 10   = 64

Displaying the calculation method in the browser.

<output> takes several attributes. **for** takes the value **element_id** to define the relationship between the elements in the calculation. **form** defines the **form_id** of the form it is embedded within. **name** gives the **<output>** a name.

<p>

The paragraph tag is one of the most common and least complicated tags there is! You simply place text between the opening and closing tags. It displays by default to block (vertical) presentation so each new paragraph will start a new line.

<picture>

The picture tag gives more nuanced control over image content. It is so nuanced that you need to nest an **<img>** element inside of **<picture>** (doesn't that sort of seem like a Christopher Nolan movie, or the Russian egg grandma dolls?? Placing an image inside of a picture….).

Inside of **<picture>** you should include **<source>** and **<img>** tags– **<img>** is required and **<source>** is merely useful. Here's an example of how you might use this construct. Let's say that you want to show an image, but you have decided to show very high-resolution gorgeous images on very large screens, but because cellular data is so slow and the screens so small, you want to serve a more highly compressed lower resolution image to handheld screens. You might code your HTML like this:

```
<picture>
  <source media="(max-width: 320px)"
srcset="https://blahblah1.jpg">
  <source media="(max-width: 720px)"
srcset="https://blahblah2.jpg">
 <source media="(min-width: 1024px)"
srcset="https://blahblah3.jpg">
  <img src="https://mainPhoto.jpg" alt="coolPhoto"
style="width:auto;">
</picture>
```

What you are doing in these lines is setting the source (**srcset** for short) to a different image, based on the condition that the viewer's screen has a maximum size dimension that you also specify. We are using "blahblah" as our URL here just for illustration purposes. blahblah1 is the lowest resolution image, blahblah2 is medium resolution, and blahblah3 is the highest resolution. You can test this easily in your browser by making each image totally different and then just change the size of your browser and watch the images change miraculously before you!

Note that the first two images are set to **max-width** values, and the third, which covers all screens from 1024px wide and upward, is set to **min-width** to capture all screens up to the largest size starting at 1024px. **<picture>** has no attributes, but is fully loaded anyway as a tag, since it needs two other tags to make it do its magic.

<pre>

Just when you thought you were getting to know the spirit of HTML, along comes a tag like **<pre>** which does NOT display content like most HTML. Do you usually need line breaks declared explicitly, such as by using **
** or organizing the content into block display elements? Yes! Do you need to worry about this in **<pre>**? Not at all. Doesn't HTML ignore white space? For sure! Does **<pre>** ignore white space? Not at all.

You may want to use **\<pre>** just to make HTML text display in the exact way that you type it in the HTML document. OR, just use it to tag content you want to target later with CSS. OR, just use it's boring default monospace courier styling. In any event, once you've experienced **\<pre>**, you will want to find endless excuses to use it!

```
<pre>Really?   Do you
actually     behave
so    oddly for an
HTML tag?</pre>
```

```
<pre>Really?   Do you
actually     behave
so    oddly for an
HTML tag?</pre>
```

\<pre> won't ignore your white space.

While **\
** allows for easily formatting online poetry because it introduces new lines wherever you want them, **\<pre>** allows for easily formatting online postmodern poetry because you can compose with empty white spaces!

\<progress>

This tag gives you a progress bar, which is sometimes shown when pages take a long time to load. To animate these in real time, you need to connect it to JavaScript and stylize it in CSS since on its own, it is pretty ugly in its raw HTML form. It takes **value** and **max** as its attributes, which are illustrated below.

```
<h2>Aren't we there yet???</h2>
<progress value="89" max="100"></progress>
```

Aren't we there yet???

The HTML raw material progress bar.

<q>

This is the quotation tag, which doesn't have a semantic quality as does `<blockquote>` since "q" is lacking in human readable content quality as a tag. The default display of `<q>` content is to wrap quotation marks around it. In the difference between the `<q>` and `<blockquote>` tags, you can get a sense of old versus new HTML standards. `<q>` is usually for short quotations and `<blockquote>` for longer ones. If you want to quote using `<q>` just wrap its opening and closing tags around your text and you're good to go!

<rp>, <rt>, <rtc> & <ruby>

These tags relate to placing some additional textual notes and characters that pertain to East Asian languages. The overall ruby expression is enclosed within the `<ruby>` tags. Within these, on can use `<rt>` to provide additional explanation or spellings in other languages, and `<rb>` to put additional contents within parentheses. `<rp>` is a fallback parenthesis that gives an alternative text for content that has characters which may not display in some browsers.

`<rtc>` is a 'ruby text container' which provides extra semantic context to the ruby content. The following code adds semantic information that is machine-readable, and that indicates the wrapped text is in English, even though other ruby elements might provide content in other languages:

```
<rtc xml:lang="en"
><rp>(</rp><rt>Trinidad!</rt><rp>)</rp></rtc>
```

The Mozilla documentation (`http://bit.ly/MozRuby`) gives this ruby example:

```
<ruby>
明日 <rp>(</rp><rt>Ashita</rt><rp>)</rp>
</ruby>
```

A use of `<ruby>` .

<s>

This is the tag that is supposed to mean "this text is not correct" because the whole concept of "strikethrough" is so HTML4, or even HTML <5. I will leave it to you whether you can detect and make use of this fine semantic distinction between a strikethrough, and a moment of incorrect text.

```
<p>This text does not have a line going through it.</p>
<p><s>There is totally a line going through this
text!</s></p>
```

This text does not have a line going through it.

~~There is totally a line going through this text!~~

\<samp\>

The sample tag functions a lot like **\<code\>** in that it is a semantic container for content that is supposed to represent the output of a computer program, which is different from the source code that might be placed within **\<code\>** tags. It defaults to monospace styling. One might use **\<code\>** and **\<samp\>** together, for instance by showing the source code within the **\<code\>** tags and then showing its output in the **\<samp\>** tags.

\<script\>

This is where you place client-side JavaScript– or script in other computer languages, which is a lot less common– to perform actions in the document. WebGL is an example of an alternative kind of script you might want to run, as it is specialized for computer graphics native to the browser, but Js is the main programming language used on HTML documents.

```
<script>
document.getElementById("goodbye").innerHTML = "Goodbye
World!";
</script>
```

This would print the opposite of "Hello World!" in a document section that has been given the **id** of "goodbye."

You can also point to an external JavaScript file with the **src** attribute, in which case your script element needs to be empty of content:

```
<script src="linkedExternalJs.js"
type="application/javascript"></script>
```

The **type** attribute is not required, but it's there if you want to use it. When you load a script into a browser as the page loads, there are three ways to load it:

- Have the script load when the browser gets to the **<script>** line(s) in the HTML document, parse the script and then continue to parse the rest of the HTML code in the document line by line. This is the default and requires no additional attribute.

- Parse the script asynchronously, meaning it will parse the script as it is also parsing the rest of the HTML document and its content. For this you need to use the **async** attribute.

- Process the script after the rest of the page loads, using the **defer** attribute. You might want to do this for faster page load times, since typically users won't start interacting with a page in the first few half seconds after the page loads.

Finally, there is a **charset** attribute if you feel that you need to use one.

<section>

If you want to divide your HTML document's content up into identifiable sections which don't necessarily have strong semantic connotations, place the content of the sections within **<section>**, which allows you to make **<section>** a parent of any of the other HTML elements you place within it.

```
<section>
    <h1>Heading</h1>
    <img>
    <p>Some paragraphs.</p>
    <p>Some paragraphs.</p>
</section>
Etc.
```

\<select\>

The select tag allows you to create a selection list, where the user is given a predefined set of options to choose from. This is different from the **\<datalist\>** tag because the user is not prompted to start typing into an input field. With **\<select\>**, there are only predefined options to select from in a popup window. **\<select\>** has the attribute **value** to define the content enclosed within its **\<option\>** tags.

```
<!DOCTYPE html>
<html>
   <body>
       <h2>Select a Bread</h2>
    <select>
      <option value="wholeWheat">Whole Wheat</option>
      <option value="white">White</option>
      <option value="sourdough">Sourdough</option>
      <option value="rye">Rye</option>
      <option value="raisinCinnamon">Raisin and
Cinnamon</option>
      <option value="pumpernickel">Pumpernickel</option>
      <option value="glutenFree">Gluten Free</option>
      <option value="marbleRye">Marble Rye</option>
    </select>
        <h2>Now Practice and Make a Pie Selection
List!</h2>
   </body>
</html>
```

Select a Bread

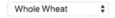

Now Practice and Make a Pie Selection List!

The construction of a basic selection list.

`<select>` has some attributes that take no additional values.
`autofocus` gives the element focus in the browser.
`disabled` will disable the affected options.
`multiple` allows users to select more than one option.
`required` makes it necessary for a user to select something in order to successfully submit the form.

Other attributes for **`<select>`** need values:

`form` requires the **`id`** of a form name.
`size` requires a number that defines the number of options in the dropdown list that will be immediately visible.

<small>

This tag allows you to structure the placement of smaller text in a document.

```
<h2>Sign this Contract!</h2>
<p>The contract sections.</p>
<p><small>The fine print where we get you.</small></p>
```

Sign this Contract!
The contract sections.
The fine print where we get you.

Using **`<small>`** *to nickel and dime your customers and enhance your bottom line.*

<source>

The source tag is used to specify different sources of media. As mentioned above in the section on **<audio>**, browsers support different audio file formats. **<source>** can be used to present a list of different audio files, for example, and the browser will select the one that matches its playback capabilities.

We have also seen an example of **<source>** working in tandem with its attribute **srcset** in the **<picture>** section above, used to change which image can display based on the devices screen size. **srcset** can thus be used to define different media files, based on what conditions are met. **src** takes a URL, either relative or absolute. **size** allows you to specify sizes, which might be keyed to layouts that adjust on different device sizes. **media** is the attribute that lets you perform media queries on the device the browser is displayed on (an example of a media query is shown above in the **<picture>** section). The **type** attribute takes as its value one of the official media types (see the full list at http://bit.ly/mediaTypes).

```
<audio controls>

  <source src="sound.ogg" type="audio/ogg">

  <source src="sound.mp3" type="audio/mpeg">

  <source src="http://soundcloud/mySound.oga"
type="audio/ogg; codecs=vorbis" />

</audio>
```

<span>

The span tag allows you to group inline elements in a document in order to do something with them, either with CSS styling or JavaScript interactions. There is no effect on the visual display simply by encasing inline elements within span tags. In addition to being a wrapper for inline elements, such as **\<img\>** and **\<button\>**, you can also create a span around text encased in heading or paragraph tags.

```
<p>Lots of text here but then <span style=".....">this
text will be styled differently and then</span> the text
will return to normal paragraph styling.</p>
```

\<span\> is sometimes considered to be the inline counterpart to **\<div\>**, which is a block element.

<strong>

The strong tag is for emphasizing important text and is used in the same way as other phrase tags, like **\<em\>** and **\<samp\>**.

<style>

The style tag is used for creating internal CSS styling in an HTML document. Internal CSS is best declared in the **\<head\>** section of the HTML document. Styles will still render if placed in the **\<body\>**, but good coding practice recommends separating the different functions of organizing the content in the **\<body\>** and styling it in the **\<head\>**. If you have more than one **\<style\>** element, they will be processed in the order presented in the HTML document, top to bottom, which means that styles applied later can overwrite styles placed above them.

In the example below, we are creating four unique **id** names, "one" and "two" for the two horizontal rules, **<hr>**, and "green" and "blue" for each **<h2>** element. We attach the internal CSS style to an **id** by using **#** after the HTML tag name.

```
<html>
  <head>
    <style>
      hr#one {
        border-top: 3px dotted green;
      }
      hr#two {
        border-top: 5px solid blue;
      }
      h2#green {
        color: green;
      }
      h2#blue {
        color: blue;
      }
    </style>
  </head>
  <body>
    <h2 id="green">Green Dotted Horizontal Rule</h2>
```

```
    <hr id="one">

    <h2 id="blue">Thick Blue Horizontal Rule</h2>

    <hr id="two">
  </body>
</html>
```

Green Dotted Horizontal Rule

....

Thick Blue Horizontal Rule

_____

Using internal CSS declared in the <head> section within the <style> tags.

`<style>` has the same media and type attributes that we've seen already for defining media devices and media types, discussed previously in tags such as `<picture>`, `<embed>` and `<source>`. Through media queries we can target speech synthesizers (**aura**l), **braille** displays, teletypes (**tty**), and projectors (**projection**). We can also target presentation aspects such as **min-width** and **max-width, orientation, device-aspect-ratio** etc. that have been presented earlier.

Media queries are a very important aspect of internal styles, since we usually want to target different devices with different layouts and other visual considerations. However, since media queries are a more advanced CSS topic, it is out of scope here and is instead covered in the companion CSS volume.

<sub>

The subscript tag allows you to place small text below the main line.

```
<p>Make sure that you drink plenty of H<sub>2</sub>O!</p>

<p>Decibels are measured in Log<sub>10</sub> or
something. Will this be on the quiz?</p>
```

Make sure that you drink plenty of H_2O!

Decibels are measured in Log_{10} or something. Will this be on the quiz?

<sub> can make your HTML documents seem more scientificky!

<sup>

Superscript is the opposite of subscript, consisting of text raised above the main line of content.

```
<p>The superscript tag makes me feel
soooo<sup>exponential</sup> !</p>
```

The superscript tag makes me feel $soooo^{exponential}$!

This script is super.

\<svg\>

This tag provides a container for scalable vector graphics. All vector graphics are scalable so the word 'scalable' is a little redundant. Raster graphics, composed of bitmaps which are the kind of images your camera takes, i.e. pixel grids, are not scalable because if you scaled them, for example by enlarging them, the pixels become more and more visible and the resolution quality decreases. In contrast, vector images are mathematically calculated out of vertices and vectors, and always display at the same resolution no matter how large or small the image is.

Here is an example of creating a circle vector image inside of **\<svg\>**, which will always have the same quality and resolution no matter how large or small it is, since it is just a mathematical rather than pixel-based rendering:

```
<svg width="250" height="250">
  <circle cx="100" cy="100" r="70" fill="salmon"
stroke="teal" stroke-width="6"/>
</svg>
```

Creating vector images inside of \<svg\>

Note that many software vector drawing and other image applications, such as Adobe Illustrator, can output any vector image with the `.svg` file extension so there are many kinds of SVG images you can embed in your document.

<table>, <tr>, <th>, <td>, <thead>, <tfoot>, & <tbody>

The construction of tables involves a number of tags that work together. A table is a two-dimensional array of rows and columns which define cells that contain information in them, called tabular data. In the early days of the web, whole page layouts used to be accomplished almost solely through clever manipulation of the table-related tags! Sometimes to illustrate key coding concepts, we need to present some very ugly examples. So, here is the hideous table we are going to create:

Vacation Excursions	
Jet Skis	$400
Dune Buggies	$300
Ancient Ruins	$30
Cenotes Tour	$250
On credit card $980	

Ugly but conceptually useful `<table>`

Before presenting the code, let's analyze its components. This whole lovely construction is nested within a parent **<table>** element. We then have three main sections for the table– its header or **<thead>** at the top ("Vacation Excursions"), its body or **<tbody>** (all the fun things to do and put on the credit card), and a footer or **<tfoot>** (keeping track of the credit pain to come later). Inside the header, there is a **<th>** (table head) for the top row of each column, which can also be thought of as a column head except that HTML doesn't use this terminology. The body has two elements nested inside it– table rows (**<tr>**, which contain pairings of excursions and pricing, and individual cells (**<td>** or table data) for each excursion and pricing content component. We have given the table's header, body and footer different styling so that you can easily distinguish each part, both in the visual reference above and in the code below.

```html
<table>
  <thead style="display: block; border: 5px solid brown ;
color: black ; background-color: aqua;">
    <tr>
      <th>Vacation</th>
      <th>Excursions</th>
    </tr>
  </thead>
  <tbody style="display: block; border: 4px solid
BlueViolet ; color: red ;">
    <tr>
      <td>Jet Skis</td>
      <td>$400</td>
    </tr>
    <tr>
      <td>Dune Buggies</td>
      <td>$300</td>
    </tr>
    <tr>
      <td>Ancient Ruins</td>
      <td>$30</td>
    </tr>
    <tr>
      <td>Cenotes Tour</td>
      <td>$250</td>
    </tr>
```

```
    </tbody>
    <tfoot style="display: block; border: dotted; 2px solid
black ; color: blue ; background-color: yellow;">
        <tr>
            <td>On credit card</td>
            <td>$980</td>
        </tr>
    </tfoot>
</table>
```

As a reminder, here we are using HTML color names, a complete list of which can be found at `http://bit.ly/MozHTMLcolor`

An optional **rowspan** attribute can be used with **<td>** and **<tr>** to offset row content by a number of columns defined in a number value.

<template>

The template tag intentionally hides content from the viewer that you want to be shown when activated by some JavaScript that is targeting it. In the Js, you would instruct the browser to reveal, or conceal after revealing, content encased inside of your **<template>**.

<textarea>

With the text area tag, you can create an area on a web page for the user to enter some text, and also specify some default text that will display when the page has loaded, and which the user can delete or overwrite. Two use cases for **<textarea>** are soliciting comments from users or allowing them to answer open ended questions in a survey. JavaScript can send this input data to the backend server or otherwise perform interactions with it.

```
<textarea rows="15" cols="20">
```

```
Here is a portrait style aspect ratio that allows the
user to enter in some text to the document. We start off
this this text which can easily be deleted once it has
loaded onto the page.
</textarea>
```

Here is a portrait style aspect ratio that allows the user to enter in some text to the document. We start off this this text which can easily be deleted once it has loaded onto the page.

An example of a textarea.

<textarea> has the following attributes:

- **autofocus** (no additional value) gives the text area focus. Focus is a small amount of the browser's computational resources to pay attention to the element in focus.

- **cols** defines how many columns wide the text area should be.

- **dirname** submits the text direction as part of the input data. It is expressed as the name of the text area (via its **name** attribute) and with **.dir** appended to it, e.g. **name.dir**

- **disabled** (no additional value) disables the text area.

- **form** takes as its value the syntax **form_id** and identifies which form(s) the text area belongs to.

- **maxlength** puts a limit on the number of characters that can be typed in a text area, so its value is the number of characters which defines the maximum limit a user is allowed to type.

- **name** gives a name for the text area, and so its value will be text.

- **placeholder** provides an option for providing some short text, as one might do when giving a hint as to what kind of data is wanted, and so its value is the placeholder text.

- **readonly** takes no additional value and makes the text area read only. This is similar to disabling the text area with **disabled**, except that disabling the element greys out the text area by default, whereas **readonly** will not grey it out.

- **required** takes no additional value and makes the input field required.

- **rows** defines the number of rows of the text area and takes a number as its value.

- **wrap** has two values, **soft** or **hard**. When the data is submitted, it can format the text as starting a new line at the places where the text reached the edge of the `<textarea>` (this would be a **hard** wrap), or it can submit the input text without inserting new lines where the words ran into the edges of the `<textarea>` (this would be a **soft** wrap).

`<time>`

The time tag allows you do format time information in your document. Time information can include clock time, calendar time or even durations. Given the importance of time generally, HTML lets you format time information either for other humans, or for computers, spider bots, web trawlers, search engines, web scrapers, rogue AI, and anything else that needs to extract machine readable information from your page. Below, time is formatted for rogue AI and the human resistance:

```
<p>Merry <time datetime="2019-12-25
07:00">Christmas!</time> Or, um, Happy Secular Holiday or
whatever. Where are the presents and cookies?</p>

<p>It is <time>10:00 pm</time>. Do you know where your
children are?</p>
```

Merry Christmas! Or, um, Happy Secular Holiday or whatever. Where are the presents and cookies?

It is 10:00 pm. Do you know where your children are?

They look exactly the same but are formatted differently for human and machine readability.

To make time machine readable, use the **datetime** attribute and set its value to a date and time. For humans who are looking at your HTML source code, or who are styling your **<time>** elements with CSS, just use plain time tags sans attribute. There are ~dozen ways you can format time 'legally' within HTML, see this link for the options:

```
http://bit.ly/legalTime
```

<title>

The title tag gives your document a title and is considered to be a required element. It displays the page's title at the top of the page in the browser tab. This will also be the default name of the page if it is saved as a bookmark, and also is used for SEO (search engine optimization). It should be placed inside the **<head>** element at the top of the HTML document.

Favicons!

A favicon is the little image icon that you typically see in the browser tab next to the title. This can be any image format (.jpg, .png, .gif etc.) but the .ico format has caught on as being very popular for favicons. You can place the favicon image in the root directory (same area as your index.html file). You then need to explicitly **<link>** to it in the **<head>** section. Here are two examples for linking to favicons. One is a jpeg file and the other an ico file.

```
<link rel="shortcut icon" type="image/x-icon"
href="favicon.ico"/>

<link rel="shortcut icon" type="image/jpeg"
href="favicon.jpg"/>
```

Recall that **type** refers to that hundreds of official Media Types mentioned earlier, and so you have to specify the formal code for your chosen media type. The `ico` format has the Media Type designation of **image/x-icon** (which you would never know without looking it up online!). **rel="shortcut icon"** defines this file as an icon so that it can be used to complement the page's **<title>** in the various functions that titles partake in, such as browser tab display and saved bookmarks.

<track>

<audio> and **<video>** might make use of **<track>** since each media format sometimes has need of other supporting files, such as subtitles or multiple channels of information. As such, **<audio>** or **<video>** will always be parents of a **<track>** element. Track takes the following attributes.

- **default** defines a default track unless overridden by user settings. It takes no additional value.

- **kind** defines text tracks, and has the values of **captions, chapters, descriptions, metadata** and **subtitles.**

- **label** takes text as its attribute and defines a name for a text track.

- **src** is required, since **<track>** has to refer to some other media file. Its value is the URL of the resource to be accessed.

- **srclang** defines that language of any text tracks and is also required for **kind="subtitle"**.

```
<video width="512" height="288" controls>

  <source src="watchVideo.mp4" type="video/mp4">

  <track src="subtitles_en.vtt" kind="subtitles"
srclang="bg" label="Bulgarian">

</video>
```

<u>

This is a very non-semantic way to underline text, because underlining with `<u>` tags doesn't say anything at all about the reasons why the text is being underlined. In HTML 5, it is actually called the 'unarticulated annotation element' which you will never remember but at least starts with a 'u'!

The original use of underlines in typography was to indicate text on a manuscript that should be italicized. So in its origins, underlined text were targeted for being stylized differently, which is a historical context that HTML5 has brought back to `<u>`. In other words, good HTML5 style asks you to have a reason to style underlined text differently, rather than just throw a line under words. But, if you want to throw a line under words, `<u>` for sure will let you do that!

<var>

The variable tag is for defining variables, which are used in both mathematics and computer programming languages, and so is similar to other phrase tags like `<code>` and `<samp>`. The default styling of `<var>` is italics.

\<video>

The video tag is the counterpart to **\<audio>** for the embedded playback of video content on a web page. It embraces a **\<source>** element which defines the video file asset.

```html
<html>

<body>

  <video width="768" height="432" controls>

     <source src="assets/video.mp4" type="video/mp4">

     <source src="assets/video.ogg" type="video/ogg">

     <source src="assets/video.webm" type="video/webm">

  </video>

</body>

</html>
```

Video content embedded in a web page.

Video media comes in different aspect ratios and codecs. For browser performance, some dimensions of the viewing window are better than others. It is recommended that you ideally aim for dimension pairings that are multiples of **16**. For video in a `16:9` aspect ratio, these might be:

`1920 x 1080`

`1024 x 576`

`512 x 288`

A second choice for aspect ratios would be those that are multiples of **8** (e.g. `384 x 216`), and third choice ratios would be multiples of **4** (e.g. `960 x 540`). There is a different set of recommended dimensions for videos shot in a `4:3` aspect ratio. This link discusses the various height and width dimensions based on these multiples,

`http://bit.ly/VidMult`

There are three video formats supported by browsers, and so you need to include links to all three kinds to ensure playback in various browsers: **MP4, Ogg** and **WebM**, as shown above, and the browser will select the best format for playback.

<video> has most of the same attributes we saw with **<audio>** earlier: **autoplay, controls, loop, muted, preload** and **src.** One attribute unique to **<video>** is **poster** which allows you to select an image that you would like to be displayed as the content loads into the browser or until the video is started. The value of **poster** is a URL to the image resource.

\<wbr>

This tag stands for 'word break opportunity' and is used typically for very long words that may need to be interrupted by formatting in the browser display. Like its cousin **\
** it is a self-closing tag. It should be inserted in the places where you might hyphenate a word as it is split to go to a new line. It produces no visual effect other than giving the browser some explicit instructions as to where there are good places to break up words and continue them on the next line.

```
<p>
The longest word in the German language is
<em>Donaudampf<wbr>schiffahrt<wbr>sgesell<wbr>schaftskapi
tän<wbr></em> and consists of 42 characters! It totally
needs wbr tags.
</p>
```

This code will render as:

The longest word in the German language is
Donaudampfschiffahrtsgesellschaftskapitän and consists of 42
characters! It totally needs wbr tags.

And that is the end of our tour of the HTML tags!

Global Attributes

In the presentations of the HTML tags above, the attributes specific to each tag have been presented and described. There is also a set of attributes called Global Attributes which apply to all HTML tags. These are shown below. Feel free to use them with any HTML tag, because they are globally available to all of them!

- **accesskey** this provides shortcuts for activating elements or bringing them into focus. One activates the shortcut key differently depending on the browser. In Chrome, it is **alt +** the **accesskey** which brings the element into focus, but in Firefox, it is **shift + alt +** the **accesskey.**

```
<!DOCTYPE html>
<html>
  <body>
    <a href="https://someURLlink..." accesskey="z">In
Chrome, focus the element w/ alt+z</a><br>
    <a href="https://someURLlink..." accesskey="x">In
Firefox, focus the element w/ shift+alt+z</a>
  </body>
</html>
```

In Chrome, focus the element w/ alt+z
In Firefox, focus the element w/ shift+alt+z

Setting up keyboard shortcuts to HTML elements to focus them.

- **autocapitalize** gives control capitalization over text input that is received from devices other than physical keyboards, e.g. voice or mobile based text inputs. Its values are:

  off or **none** no capitalization is applied.
  on or **sentences** will capitalize the first letter of a sentence.
  words the first letter of every word will be capitalized.
  characters all letters will be in uppercase.

- **class** class names can be assigned to any elements to show that they have a special function that applies to more than one of them. The main uses of the **class** attribute are to reference a group HTML elements in a stylesheet, or to manipulate them with JavaScript.

- **contenteditable** clarifies whether an element can be edited or not. It takes the values **true** or **false.**

```
<!DOCTYPE html>
<html>
  <body>
    <p contenteditable="true">
      Please click on me and change what I say.
    </p>
  </body>
</html>
```

Please click on me and change what I say.

Content that is editable can be changed in the webpage.

- **data-*** stores customized data that is private to the web page or an application. In the course of our website project, we may wish to create our own custom data labels, hierarchies or classification schemes, to be used by Js or CSS scripts, for example.

```
<!DOCTYPE html>
<html>
  <h1 data-song-genre="hiphop">Dear Mama</h1>
  <h1 data-song-genre="edm">Levels</h1>
  <h1 data-song-genre="folkrock">Like a Rolling
Stone</h1>
</html>
```

Dear Mama
Levels
Like a Rolling Stone

An example of giving customized data to HTML elements, which can be used by JavaScript or CSS.

- **dir** gives the direction of text progression for an element with textual content. The three values **dir** takes are **ltr** (left-to-right), **rtl** (right-to-left) and **auto** (let the browser decide). This is illustrated above in the section on the **<bdo>** tag.

- **draggable** Have you ever tried to drag a photo from a website onto your desktop and found out that you couldn't? This attribute controls whether or not an element is draggable and takes as its values **true** or **false**. In the example below, you will not be able to drag the image from a web page onto your computer's desktop.

```
<!DOCTYPE html>
<html>
  <body>
    <img src="http://bit.ly/33y4EuS" width="300"
height="300" alt="city" draggable="false">
  </body>
</html>
```

- **dropzone** is a new global attribute and is not currently supported by most browsers. It indicates the kinds of content that can be dropped onto an element and uses the HTML Drag and Drop API. It takes the values **move, copy** or **link**.

- **hidden** controls the visibility and relevance of an element. It can keep content from being displayed until some condition is met in Js which can then remove this attribute and make the element visible. It takes no value other than itself.

- **id** this provides unique identifiers to elements that are a special case of some kind. These identifiers can be utilized by Js or CSS for interaction or stylization purposes or used by in-page anchors for internal navigation on the same page. The value is a unique name.

- **inputmode** allows for inputs to be designed that are optimized for certain kinds of data entry. Its possible values are:

  none used when the page has its own keyboard feature.
  text is the default for receiving keyboard-based data.
  decimal includes number formatting for decimals and large numbers by providing periods and commas.
  numeric expects data from a numerical entry keypad, with numbers ranging 0-9.
  tel optimizes data entry for phone numbers, including characters for * , # and -
  search optimizes data for performing a search function.
  email formatting includes the character @ to helps with entering emails.
  url is optimized for web addresses and includes http and domain elements built in.

- **itemprop** allows you to add unique item properties to an element of your own devising, similar to **id** and **class**.

```
<h1 itemprop="Vietnamese">Pho</h1>
<h1 itemprop="Mexican">Enchilada</h1>
<h1 itemprop="Greek">Moussaka</h1>
<h1 itemprop="Polish">Pierogi</h1>
```

Pho

Enchilada

Moussaka

Pierogi

There isn't any visual change with using itemprop, but this attribute allows code to search out custom properties given to HTML elements.

- **lang** indicates an element's language the two-letter language codes.

- **spellcheck** specifies whether or not an element's spelling and grammar should be checked

```
<!DOCTYPE html>
<html>
  <body>
    <h3>Red Dots Under Misspelled Words</h3>
    <form>
      <p>
        <input type="text" spellcheck="true">
      </p>
      <button type="submit">Send Our Way!</button>
    </form>
  </body>
</html>
```

Red Dots Under Misspelled Words

helo thare

Send Our Way!

Yes, that's right, the browser can check your spelling, too!

- **style** provides a place for inline CSS styling within the tag. It's syntax is:

  ```
  <tag style="property:value;  property:value; property:value">
  ```

- **tabindex** gives an element's tabbing order. This allows users to tab quickly through a site's tabbable content, using the keyboard's tab key. For example, you might want a user to tab through items on a form, or across images to select them. It takes the value of the tabbing order, e.g. **1, 2, 3, 4** etc.

- **title** provides additional information about an element that may be relevant and will display a popup box when the cursor moves over it. One of its most common uses is to provide tips or help comments over items as the user expresses interest in them by placing the cursor over it.

- **translate** indicates whether an element should be subject to translation or not, and delivers this information to the browser by taking values of **yes** or **no**.

Tags by Category

The tags have been presented alphabetically so that they can be found quickly when this book is used as a reference. Tags can also be grouped by their general function, which is shown below. The groupings below are taken from the HTML Standard website,

```
http://bit.ly/HTMLstandard
```

General HTML Document

```
<html>
<head>
<title>
<base>
<link>
<meta>
<style>
```

Sections

```
<body>
<article>
<section>
<nav>
<aside>
<h1, h2, h3, h4, h5, h6>
<hgroup>
<header>
<footer>
<address>
```

Grouping

```
<p>
<hr>
<pre>
<blockquote>
<ol>
<ul>
<menu> (note: this only works in Firefox so is not
covered in this book)
<li>
<dl>
<dt>
<dd>
<figure>
<figcaption>
<main>
<div>
```

Text Semantics

```
<a>
<em>
<strong>
<small>
<s>
<cite>
<q>
<dfn>
<abbr>
<ruby>
<rt>
<rp>
<data>
<time>
<code>
<var>
<samp>
<kbd>
```

```
<sub>
<sup>
<i>
<b>
<u>
<mark>
<bdi>
<bdo>
<span>
<br>
<wbr>
```

Links

```
<a>
<area>
```

Edits

```
<ins>
<del>
```

Embedded Content

```
<picture>
<source>
<img>
<iframe>
<embed>
<object>
<param>
<video>
<audio>
<track>
<map>
<area>
```

Tables

```
<table>
<caption>
<colgroup>
<col>
<tbody>
<thead>
<tfoot>
<tr>
<td>
<th>
```

Forms

```
<form>
<label>
<input>
<button>
<select>
<datalist>
<optgroup>
<option>
<textarea>
<output>
<option>
<textarea>
<output>
<progress>
<meter>
<fieldset>
<legend>
```

Interactive

```
<details>
<summary>
```

Scripting

\<script\>
\<noscript\>
\<template\>
\<slot\>
\<canvas\>

Code Validation

Code validation is the process of having your code checked for errors and deviations from the standard. There are online tools you can use to check your HTML code for any problem areas. These services can be found via a simple search engine return on "HTML code validator." Some code validators ask you to upload an HTML file or paste in the HTML code. Others accept the URL of the live website and can check your code from its presence on the web. A code validation result will seek out potential problem areas in your code and indicate these as either Warnings or Errors, depending on the severity of the code wobbliness. Also, the message will indicate the exact line and column of the code where the error can be found, or the range of lines where the wobbliness is propagating.

Here are the kinds of messages a code validator might return to you after checking your code:

```
Warning: Consider adding a lang attribute to the html
start tag to declare the language of this document. From
line 6, column 4; to line 7, column 6
```

```
Warning: Consider avoiding viewport values that prevent
users from resizing documents. From line 21, column 3; to
line 21, column 90
```

```
Warning: Section lacks heading. Consider using h2-h6
elements to add identifying headings to all sections.
From line 72, column 8; to line 72, column 30
```

```
Error: An img element must have an alt attribute, except
under certain conditions. For details, consult guidance
on providing text alternatives for images. From line 248,
column 9; to line 248, column 60
```

Developer Tools

You can right click on any web page and small popup window with a variety of options will appear. Our interest in this section is with the View Source and Inspection options. Most websites are fairly complicated to view in these tools, and unless you have a certain degree of coding competency, it is probably not very useful to stare at long lines of code you don't understand, not to mention the deep developer tool sets which are for more experienced developers.

However, you should at least know about these tools and start to noodle around with them, especially on your own websites which in the beginning of your coding journey will probably be far less complicated than most professional ones. If you open your website in any browser and right click anywhere on it, you will see options to View Source and Inspect. View Source will show the source code of the page, whereas Inspect opens up a robust suite of developer tools. In an inspector, you can make temporary modifications to your code that don't change the source code in the files, but only its rendering in the browser, which gives you some freedom to experiment with your code without actually modifying the source files. You can always return to the original display of your source code just by hitting the refresh button on the browser.

The exact terminology and tools used by different browsers is a bit different. Firefox and Chrome both use View Source in their pop-up menu on a web page right-click, but for accessing the developer tools, Firefox uses "Inspect Element" whereas Chrome uses "Inspect."

Once inside the developer tools, there are other similarities and differences. Chrome has a list of tool set tabs called `Elements, Console, Sources, Network, Performance, Memory, Application, Security` etc. Firefox's developer tabs are `Inspector, Console, Debugger, Network, Style Editor, Performance, Memory, Storage, Accessibility` etc. So if you want to start diving into developer tools, choose one of these to start with, so you don't become confused by these browser-specific differences.

Exploring your web projects though the developer tools will give you new insights into structural features of your pages as well as how your site works within the overall systems architecture of the web and internet. As you progress through developing skills, you will find these tools to be of increasing interest.

List of All Bit.ly Links Used

`http://bit.ly/allCode`
All code examples.

`http://bit.ly/specChar`
List of special characters and their html codes.

`http://bit.ly/ISOlangCode`
ISO 639-1 two-letter language codes.

`http://bit.ly/linkATTR`
List of `rel` values for the `<a>` tag.

`http://bit.ly/mediaTypes`
List of all the different Media Types.

`http://bit.ly/SandboxAllow`
List of restrictions that can be removed via the sandbox attribute.

`http://bit.ly/33y4EuS`
Image of a cityscape used in various examples.

http://bit.ly/allowFeatures
Feature list for **allow** attribute.

http://bit.ly/objCite
Use of **<object>** tag (because it is so easily confused with **<embed>** !).

http://bit.ly/MozOutput
Mozilla developer site page on the **<output>** tag.

http://bit.ly/MozRuby
Mozilla **<ruby>** documentation.

http://bit.ly/MozHTMLcolor
Mozilla color name list.

http://bit.ly/legalTime
Mozilla resource for the various HTML legal ways to define the **datetime** attribute.

http://bit.ly/HTMLstandard
The official HTML Standard.

http://bit.ly/PLOScow
PLOS One cow article.

http://bit.ly/VidMult
Resource for deciding on optimal dimensions for video files.

Where to Go Next

Now that you've got a solid understanding of HTML5, the next step in your web design journey is the companion volume to this one, *CSS3 Visual Learning Guide:*
a comprehensive example set for getting up to speed fast.

Image Credits

Here and there a few images from open access stock photo sites were used. These images require no attribution, and so a thank you to the creators is hereby being sent in lieu of a photo credit.

Online Resources

There are hundreds of great online resources that you can use as a reference for diving deeper into the granular aspects of HTML tags, attributes and values, not to mention all the ways HTML can interface with JavaScript, APIs, servers and web applications. Here are a selected few to get you started down the path of deeper reference explorations.

HTML the Living Standard
```
https://html.spec.whatwg.org/
```

Mozilla Developer Network HTML Reference
```
https://developer.mozilla.org/en-
US/docs/Web/HTML/Reference
```

W3 Schools HTML Reference
```
https://www.w3schools.com/tags/
```

About the Author

Mike Ludo is a developer, educator and entrepreneur based in Seattle, Washington.

Please Write a Review

Amazon reviews are encouraged. Constructive feedback can be emailed to mike@mikeludo.com I am confident that you have learned much if you have worked through the examples in the book by accessing the online code, since this method of learning is 'battle tested' over the many years of its application.